ADVANCED PRAISE FOR

THE TRANSPOSED MUSICIAN

"This book asks and explores fascinating questions about what it means to study music in a changing world. Are there skills we can learn in our music lessons which can enrich our lives in other, non-musical areas, and then can we bring those expanded skills back into our study of music itself? Too often our conservatories are dead-ends, stuck with outdated, one-dimensional approaches which can lead to stunted personal development. This book suggests ways in which we can break down doors, for students and teachers alike, and celebrate music as something life-affirming, in and out of the studio."

—Stephen Hough
Pianist, Composer, Writer

"… In his new book entitled *The Transposed Musician*, Professor Dylan Savage…identifies eight of these benefits—Problem-Solving, Focus, Patience, Critical-Thinking, Communication, Collaboration, Improvisation, and Creativity—and calls them "universal skills" which may be developed consciously and systematically within the context of traditional music lessons. Doing so takes what has been implicit all along and makes it explicit. Music is good for us! Music teachers, even at the highest conservatory level, learn from Professor Savage that they are not so much professional trainers as guides to a happier, more successful life."

—Dr. Joseph Robinson
Principal Oboe, New York Philharmonic (1978-2005)
Author, Teacher, Producer, and Arts Advocate

"*The Transposed Musician* is an important contribution to our literature on teaching essential life skills including problem-solving, patience, focus, critical thinking, and creativity within the traditional music lesson. Teachers and students both can benefit from the study and application of these skills."

—Jane Magrath
Pianist, Author, Composer
University of Oklahoma

"In *The Transposed Musician*, Dylan Savage combines a visionary's deep understanding of the challenges music students and teachers face with an eminently practical way to meet those challenges. Using a master teacher's insight, Savage "transposes" eight potential stumbling blocks into eight universal skills that can be acquired through a beautifully organized, step-by-step approach. In turn, he shows how these skills can be applied to other areas in our rapidly changing world, helping us lead more satisfying, meaningful, and fulfilling lives, not only as musicians, but as human beings. For students and teachers alike, an inspired and inspiring book."

—Barbara Lister-Sink, Ed.D.
Producer, Freeing the Caged Bird – Developing Well Coordinated, Injury – Preventive Piano Technique

"Dylan Savage has given us a fresh and creative pedagogy to guide our music students toward life as 21st century musicians. … I really think this is an important and helpful book with a point of view that is much needed. The empathy and knowledge of the author steer the reader toward the realities of today's musical world, a world that requires skilled musicians to have universal skills that benefit their lives, regardless of their ultimate career paths."

—Phyllis Alpert Lehrer
Professor Emerita
Westminster Choir College of Rider University
Artist Faculty, Westminster Conservatory

"Dylan Savage's use of universal skills transforms music teaching into a viable and essential part of education in the 21st century. This book challenges many preconceived ideas about teaching music and mastering performance. Bravo to this new, revolutionary approach to teaching music efficiently and preparing students to successfully thrive in our modern, competitive market-place."

—Randall Hartsell
Composer, Clinician, and Teacher

THE
TRANSPOSED
MUSICIAN

TEACHING UNIVERSAL SKILLS
TO IMPROVE PERFORMANCE
AND BENEFIT LIFE

THE TRANSPOSED MUSICIAN

TEACHING UNIVERSAL SKILLS
TO IMPROVE PERFORMANCE
AND BENEFIT LIFE

DYLAN SAVAGE

GIA Publications, Inc.
Chicago

G-10049
ISBN: 978-1-62277-433-3

GIA Publications, Inc.
7404 S. Mason Ave.
Chicago, IL 60638
www.giamusic.com

Cover art by Andrew Schultz
Layout by Martha Chlipala
Edited by Jennifer Kerr Budziak

Printed in the United States of America.

For my wife,

Susan Savage,

whose wonderful support and amazing organizational skills

helped me immeasurably in the writing of this book.

Acknowledgements

My sincere thanks to Alec Harris, who said yes to this book,

and to my editor,
Jennifer Kerr Budziak, for her fine, critical work behind the scenes.

TABLE OF CONTENTS

INTRODUCTION. 13

CHAPTER ONE: Problem-Solving 29

   I.   Skill Importance, Context, Definition, and Breakdown 30

  II. Tonic Key—*Learn to Apply the Skill to Music* 32

 III. Pivot Chord—*Prepare to Transpose the Skill to a Non-Music*

      Application 43

 IV. Transposition—*Actively Transpose the Skill to a Non-Music*

      Application 44

  V. Recap—*Revisit the Skill in Music* 49

 VI. Questions for Reflection 50

 VII. Suggested Reading .50

VIII. References 51

 IX. Notes 52

CHAPTER TWO: Focus. 53

   I.   Skill Importance, Context, Definition, and Breakdown 54

  II. Tonic Key—*Learn to Apply the Skill to Music* 59

 III. Pivot Chord—*Prepare to Transpose the Skill to a Non-Music*

      Application 68

IV.   Transposition—*Actively Transpose the Skill to a Non-Music Application* 73

  V.   Recap—*Revisit the Skill in Music* 75

 VI.   Questions for Reflection 77

VII.   Suggested Reading 77

VIII. References 78

 IX.   Notes 79

CHAPTER THREE: Patience. 81

   I.   Skill Importance, Context, Definition, and Breakdown 82

  II.   Tonic Key—*Learn to Apply the Skill to Music* 85

 III.   Pivot Chord—*Prepare to Transpose the Skill to a Non-Music Application* 89

  IV.   Transposition—*Actively Transpose the Skill to a Non-Music Application* 91

   V.   Recap—*Revisit the Skill in Music* 94

  VI.   Questions for Reflection 95

 VII.   Suggested Reading 95

VIII.   References 96

  IX.   Notes 97

CHAPTER FOUR: Critical Thinking 99

   I.   Skill Importance, Context, Definition, and Breakdown 100

  II.   Tonic Key—*Learn to Apply the Skill to Music* 105

 III.   Pivot Chord—*Prepare to Transpose the Skill to a Non-Music Application* 111

  IV.   Transposition—*Actively Transpose the Skill to a Non-Music Application* 112

   V.   Recap—*Revisit the Skill in Music* 116

VI. Questions for Reflection 117

VII. Suggested Reading 118

VIII. References 118

IX. Notes 119

CHAPTER FIVE: Communication 121

I. Skill Importance, Context, Definition, and Breakdown 122

II. Tonic Key—*Learn to Apply the Skill to Music* 128

III. Pivot Chord—*Prepare to Transpose the Skill to a Non-Music*
     Application 145

IV. Transposition—*Actively Transpose the Skill to a Non-Music*
     Application 146

V. Recap—*Revisit the Skill in Music* 151

VI. Questions for Reflection 152

VII. Suggested Reading 152

VIII. References 153

IX. Notes 154

CHAPTER SIX: Collaboration 155

I. Skill Importance, Context, Definition, and Breakdown 156

II. Tonic Key—*Learn to Apply the Skill to Music* 160

III. Pivot Chord—*Prepare to Transpose the Skill to a Non-Music*
     Application 167

IV. Transposition—*Actively Transpose the Skill to a Non-Music*
     Application 169

V. Recap—*Revisit the Skill in Music* 173

VI. Questions for Reflection 173

VII. Suggested Reading 174

VIII. References 174

IX. Notes 175

CHAPTER SEVEN: Improvisation. 177

   I.   Skill Importance, Context, Definition, and Breakdown 178

   II. Tonic Key—*Learn to Apply the Skill to Music* 186

   III. Pivot Chord—*Prepare to Transpose the Skill to a Non-Music Application* 190

   IV. Transposition—*Actively Transpose the Skill to a Non-Music Application* 191

   V.   Recap—*Revisit the Skill in Music* 198

   VI. Questions for Reflection 198

   VII. Suggested Reading 199

   VIII. References 200

   IX. Notes 202

CHAPTER EIGHT: Creativity 203

   I.   Skill Importance, Context, Definition, and Breakdown 204

   II. Tonic Key—*Learn to Apply the Skill to Music* 210

   III. Pivot Chord—*Prepare to Transpose the Skill to a Non-Music Application* 233

   IV. Transposition—*Actively Transpose the Skill to a Non-Music Application* 235

   V.   Recap—*Revisit the Skill in Music* 244

   VI. Questions for Reflection 245

   VII. Suggested Reading 245

   VIII. References 246

   IX. Notes 247

CHAPTER NINE: Benefits to Teachers 249

   I.   References 265

   II. Notes 266

POSTSCRIPT 267

ABOUT THE AUTHOR 277

INTRODUCTION

THE PREMISE

The Transposed Musician is a practical guide for teaching universal skills within the context of the traditional music lesson. Eight skills have been chosen for the purposes of this book: problem-solving, focus, patience, critical thinking, communication, collaboration, improvisation, and creativity. These skills are critical to preparing music students to confront the challenges of 21st century careers because they serve a dual purpose: they can significantly improve students' music performance levels and simultaneously benefit many other aspects of their lives as well. In my experience, students practice and perform better after comprehensively learning and applying universal skills. Further, because legions of music students ultimately go on to blended or non-music careers, this new approach broadens the purpose and viability of studying music because students can comprehensively learn and apply skills that are *universal tools,* good for nearly any application. This teachers' guide is based upon the approach to teaching and applying universal skills in the music lesson that I have developed and used in my university piano teaching over the last two decades.

The Transposed Musician shows how to teach universal skills: first, through the music-making process, and second, how to transfer or "transpose" those skills to non-music applications. Music teachers need not have any particular expertise with non-music topics in order to succeed. By guiding students with thought-provoking questions, music teachers can inspire their students to "transpose" each skill outside the lesson on the students' own time. Using this method, my own students understand a skill on a deeper and more comprehensive level when they apply it in multiple disciplines or situations. The beauty of this approach is that universal skills, applied in multiple settings, circle back to further reinforce students' musical abilities. Hence, *The Transposed Musician* approach is an active cross-training of universal skills.

This cross-training method of applying those universal skills to new, non-music situations builds stronger musicians with more all-around capabilities in life as well. We know that a melody is transposed by taking it to a new key area and the music is more fully developed as a result. Similarly, a musician is "transposed" when they apply (take) a universal skill to a new area outside the field of music and the skill is more fully developed as a result. Universal skill fluency helps the transposed musician to build a more versatile and functional toolkit for all of life.

JUST HOW WELL DO OUR STUDENTS DEVELOP UNIVERSAL SKILLS ON THEIR OWN?

Music teachers have often said that their students don't just learn to play music; they also obtain universal life skills along the way. However, that's only partially true because students are largely left to learn those skills *on their own* and often not very effectively. That's because we spend most of our time helping our students with music proficiency, not on universal skills. What music method advocates comprehensive universal skill learning? I do not know of any. In my decades of piano teaching, reading, speaking with colleagues across the U.S., and attending dozens of music conferences, I have never encountered an article, discussion, paper, or book in which universal skills are either proposed or shown how to be taught systematically in the music lesson. Further, while I earned three degrees in two top music institutions in the United States (Oberlin and Indiana University), never once were any of the universal skills mentioned as something to be learned and applied. Of course, there was the occasional directive, such as: "You need to focus more intensely in this section" or "Try to be more creative with that phrase." It seems clear, then, that we have largely left the learning of universal skills for our students to develop on their own. Yet not only are these tools critically important to learning an instrument well, but their importance to countless other disciplines and applications can't be overstated.

UNTAPPED RESOURCES

Universal skills, then, are an untapped goldmine that we have neglected. We have assumed those skills will be learned well on their own. That's because we have largely presumed and commonly touted them to be automatic by-products of music studies. This is not the case, however. Although universal skills *are* inherent and necessary in the study of music, the longstanding (and mistaken) belief that these skills develop naturally and transfer themselves automatically to other applications and disciplines leaves this critical learning process entirely up to chance. In my observations, universal skills that are randomly self-learned in the context of the music lesson are usually mere shadows of the fully realized version of skills learned systematically with *conscious intent*. This book is my answer to this pressing need.

THE TRADITIONAL MUSIC LESSON IS NOT DISRUPTED OR DISPLACED

How does *The Transposed Musician* offer an effective, systematic approach for how to teach universal skills in the music lesson and also how to transfer them to other uses *without* disrupting the music lesson? This method is easily incorporated into the structure of the existing traditional lesson, as the following chapters will demonstrate. How much you choose to infuse universal skill training into each lesson is entirely up to you and the needs of your student. Universal skills should be thought of in the same vein as music theory, music history, music wellness, and music entrepreneurship—as a necessary component to becoming a well-rounded and competent musician.

UNIVERSAL SKILLS ARE MEGA-TOOLS

Many of the skills taught in this book have been deemed so important that they are routinely found at the top of lists that colleges and universities most want their students to learn (problem-solving, creativity, communication, critical thinking, etc.). Those same skills are also the ones that business and industry desire most in their employees. Because these skills are so universal in application, the idea of transference is central to *The Transposed Musician*. When a student exercises a skill in multiple areas, it is understood at a much deeper level—this is the great benefit of cross-training and the concept of intersectionality (how the same basic skill or idea functions across various disciplines). This process simultaneously improves musical performance and more thoroughly prepares the student for life, no matter where music takes them. In my estimation, this is a win-win proposition! And by doing so, it increases the relevance, value, and impact of the music lesson, *without displacing the traditional music curriculum.*

Today's music students need universal skill training as a significant part of their study diet in order to succeed, regardless of their eventual career path. Universal skill training can be started early, as soon as a student's cognitive ability allows—with the teacher carefully adjusting the necessary levels of nuance and intensity as necessary. Universal skill acquisition and competency is at the very heart of this book. It needs to be stated again that these skills can greatly benefit instrument proficiency as well as proficiency in non-music disciplines (you can actually have your cake and eat it too). In my experience, students perform better in music (and in non-music areas) when universal skills are comprehensively learned and applied.

BENEFITS TO STUDENTS

Imagine the benefits to your students' performances when they begin to employ a universal skill, such as critical thinking, taught comprehensively in their lessons with you. Then think of how the boundaries of the traditional music lesson are expanded still more when you show them how to actively transfer the same skill to non-music areas at will. Do you think your sphere of influence and impact on your students' lives and careers will have been increased? I believe dramatically so. Finally, imagine the outcome if many of those skills were systematically taught and transferred as a natural and integral part of the music lesson! Those skills now become effective and reliable tools, beneficial to *all* aspects of your music students' endeavors over the course of their entire lives. *The Transposed Musician* approach enables students to apply skills immediately and more effectively to both music and other disciplines or careers. In my experience, this ability to transpose universal skills across disciplines—via active cross-training—promotes indelible learning and helps to ensure adaptability throughout life. The end result: music students benefit *no matter what career path they ultimately take, music or non-music.*

BENEFITS TO TEACHERS— A GREATER SENSE OF PURPOSE

Teachers will benefit, too, because, using this new approach, they now have the potential to simultaneously give students the tools and skills to be better musicians *and* teach them to transpose those same skills into "gold" that can be spent almost anywhere.

For me, this approach has translated into giving me a deeper sense of purpose and satisfaction with the work I do with my students: I have not only helped them become better musicians, but I have given them tools that will serve them capably throughout the full spectrum of their lives. That realization dramatically expanded my notion of the music lesson. *The Transposed Musician* approach can translate into sending your students into the world even more enriched, empowered, and capable. I hope music teachers will be attracted to this new approach and excited by the possibilities it creates for the music studio.

BENEFITS TO MUSIC DEPARTMENTS AND SCHOOLS

In the bigger picture, music schools and departments will benefit because this *evolution of purpose* for the music lesson can serve to enrich and revitalize the mission of the curriculum. In that scenario, music lessons serve as a fulcrum to learn and leverage universal skills, preparing music students for those blended or non-music careers which are becoming more and more a reality, even for the very best of our music students. Furthermore, this evolution of purpose can fulfill an existential need in the world of applied music instruction: to update and revalidate the viability of the study of music. This will include integrative learning because this universal skill method challenges students to make connections across disciplines, helping them become better innovators, communicators, and music advocates. I believe this evolution of purpose is crucial to the reversal of shrinking enrollments now commonly found in music higher education.

THE CURRENT STATE OF AFFAIRS IS AN INCREASING CONCERN

Currently, the Western European, 19th century conservatory model of music training, used the world over, is highly music performance-based. That model, however, has become increasingly problematic and outdated because it ignores the new and different demands of the 21st century job marketplace. Students now need significant competency not only in the ability to perform on their instrument, but in other areas as well. Leading music educators know that the existing private-lesson model no longer fully addresses the needs of students today, as evidenced by the focus of national conferences such as a recent

College Music Society pre-conference workshop entitled "The End of the Conservatory"[1] and the University of South Carolina's "21st Century Music School Design."[2] In each, conversations revolved around questions such as: where do we go from here, how do we better-prepare our music students, and how do we design relevant, thriving 21st-century music programs?

Recently, William Quillen, the Oberlin Conservatory's acting dean, said, "Every conservatory is having this conversation. The realities of being a professional musician are completely different from the world of 2010 or 2000, let alone 1980…What we offer them in 2020 has to be different—and will invariably and must be different, from what we offered them 10, 20, 30, 40 years ago."[3]

Many of us know exactly what realities Quillen is referring to: graduating students are sent out into a world in which traditional music job opportunities are shrinking, and where the challenges to developing any kind of career in music are increasing dramatically. Consequently, students need to have a new, expanded knowledge base compared to what they were taught even a few decades ago. In response, there are a growing number of books which address many of these new and necessary knowledge base areas, including: entrepreneurship, wellness, music advocacy, etc. However, for those areas of knowledge to function at their fullest, something else is needed.

What this book presents is something quite different from the fairly recent topics mentioned above and yet, at the same time, just as necessary. *The Transposed Musician* fills a missing and vital link: comprehensive universal skill competency. It is something *very much needed* by students if they are to obtain the maximum results from any application, including the topics just listed. For example, how can a student extract the most from their entrepreneurship training without good problem-solving, creativity, focus, patience, communication, critical thinking, improvisation, and collaborative skills? It bears repeating: these critical, underlying skills are the bedrock of doing *anything* well and with sustainability.

One of the primary questions music educators are now asking is: what do our students need most? Even though answers vary, I think most would agree that students need *tools* that serve them well in multiple situations and varied careers—and that is exactly what universal skills do. If, for example, students learn to apply the skill of communication to performing on their instrument, and then they learn how to transfer the same skill to speaking and writing, they are far more prepared when life requires that particular skill. They are also learning to apply skills and concepts across boundaries. Transference is a major part of this book and it offers an answer to the primary question music educators are asking—what do our students need right now? *The Transposed Musician* satisfies that need by offering a new approach that advocates teaching transferrable, universal skills as a *foundation* in the music lesson, not as an occasional passing reference.

The Indiana University SNAAP study (Strategic National Arts Alumni Project) shows that our graduating musicians are supporting themselves in a wide variety of ways; more often than not in fields *other* than music. That data only further reinforces the need for systematic and in-depth universal skill training. (Chapter Nine, Benefits to Teachers, contains numerous citations from this study.)

A TOUCHY SUBJECT

In music higher education, there have been murmurings, private conversations, and even very public addresses by concerned music professors about the ethical question of continuing to mint so many highly specialized music performance degrees with so few job opportunities available. This concern was clearly alluded to in *Clavier Companion* by Robert Weirich in 2018 in his "Winds of Change" column where he wrote, "Music schools have not really changed in a century, modeled as they are on the European conservatory of the 19th century…Yet there is intense competition among them…indeed for any student to fill the teaching loads of the tenured faculty."[4] Yoheved Kaplinsky, chair of the piano department at Juilliard, said to a large audience during an address at the 2005 World Piano Pedagogy Conference[5] that she encourages all her prospective piano students *not* to seek a career in music unless they cannot imagine doing anything else. Obviously, we music teachers are grappling with a dilemma.

Not surprisingly, we are not the only discipline facing this dilemma: a recent Chronicle of Higher Education article highlighted Columbia University's English Ph.D. program and its struggle to place its graduates in higher education jobs.[6] Concerned students wrote a letter to their department leadership asking for "meaningful, measurable steps" to be taken to address this concern. Among the responses, one in particular very clearly hints at what I am advocating: "…it is vital for departments like Columbia and Yale to think about how the training that's specific to obtaining a Ph.D. in English might provide skills that lend themselves to jobs off the tenure-track, or outside university walls altogether."[7] Surely those skills must include universal skills! *The Transposed Musician* directly addresses the same concern facing administrators in music higher education by introducing an evolution of purpose for music teachers and professors to consider: integrating comprehensive universal skill training into the music lesson to broaden students' employment options, including those *within* their disciplines. This approach may help relieve some of those ethical burdens because it can better prepare students for hybrid or alternative career possibilities. By providing your students with comprehensive universal skill training in the music lesson, you can feel assured that you have given them highly functional and *adaptive* tools for their future.

IMPLEMENTATION

Let's further explore the idea that universal skill competency can improve performance levels of musicians. For example, a comprehensive understanding of **problem-solving** steps enables musicians to identify areas in their playing where refinement is needed more quickly and accurately. It also allows them to create better strategies on how to most efficiently improve those areas. This skill can lead to faster, more accurate and solid learning. The chapter on **focus** provides exercises and strategies to develop the mind's ability to remain on task for extended periods in order to improve learning efficiency and performing under pressure. The **creativity** chapter targets the interpretive elements of music-making by providing musicians a new way of thinking about and developing that elusive element we call musical expression. This skill, practiced in the steps advocated in this book, can help musicians both develop an individual voice and generate ideas to more effectively engage their audiences. The chapter on **improvisation** helps students become more comfortable with the element of change and the opportunities those changes may present. In innumerable ways, well-learned and applied universal skills can greatly benefit music proficiency and performance levels.

Let's also further pursue the idea that universal skills, first learned in the music lesson, can also greatly benefit *non*-music disciplines. As most music teachers know, a great number of our music students do not go on to careers in music. There are many reasons for this. Some simply cannot achieve a high enough level. Some do, but hit the supply and demand ceiling where there are simply far more musicians than music jobs; in those cases, non-music (or blended) careers often become the only alternative. In addition, plenty of talented students with significant music backgrounds ultimately prefer other careers. Those realities will only increase if we continue to direct our energies to primarily teaching our students music proficiency (the old Western European Conservatory way). However, I hope you can now see an opportunity to extend the range of benefits offered by the traditional music studio. Wouldn't it be satisfying to the profession and present huge growth possibilities if music lessons resolutely required comprehensive universal skill learning, tailored to better help students for *any* endeavor or discipline?

To further extend the idea of using music study as a vehicle to train universal skills, what if some students took music lessons or a music course (or two) for the *primary* reason of improving their chances to excel in careers other than music? Perhaps they might have been attracted to a private teacher who advertised lessons with universal skills as the primary component, or a university that offered a course called Universal Skill-Building through Music Performance.

Wouldn't that be novel! Could that course become a new offering and perhaps even a field of study? I think those possibilities are very real and much needed.

LAYOUT

The layout of this guide book is user-friendly. There is no set order to these chapters, allowing music teachers to pick whatever skill chapter seems most relevant to the needs of a particular student at a given moment. *Because of this self-contained chapter design, there will be some repetition throughout the book in explaining concepts and skills.* Each skill chapter is laid out in a like manner, so the teacher knows exactly where to find what they need at any given time:

   I.   **Skill Importance, Context, Definition, and Breakdown**

   II.   **Tonic Key—***Learn to Apply the Skill to Music*

   III.   **Pivot Chord—***Prepare to Transpose the Skill to a Non-Music Application*

   IV.   **Transposition—***Actively Transpose the Skill to a Non-Music Application*

   V.   **Recap—***Revisit the Skill in Music*

   VI.   **Questions for Reflection**

   VII.   **Suggested Reading**

   VIII.   **References**

   IX.   **Notes**

Each of the eight skill chapters begins with **Skill Importance, Context, Definition,** and **Breakdown** so there is no question as to what the skills are, their function, and purpose. Then, in the section called "**Tonic Key,**" the method of how to apply the skill in the music lesson is shown through a series of steps for the specific purpose of improving the student's ability on their instrument. Next, once a skill is well-understood and the student has successfully applied and practiced it at their instrument, the **"Pivot Chord"** helps the teacher ask a few questions of the student to get them thinking about how the skill can be transferred ("transposed") to benefit them in a non-music area of the student's own choosing. It is important to mention here that the teacher needs no special knowledge of any non-music area in order to accomplish this. Then, in the section called **"Transposition,"** examples are given to illustrate possible conversations to have in the lesson. Later, the student puts the skill into use *outside* the lesson itself for active learning for the specific purpose of benefiting an academic class, project, or job. Here, the same systematic steps for applying the skill in the tonic key (the music application) are followed. In **"Recap,"** the teacher further reinforces the skill in the lesson by briefly reviewing, with the student, its application to music. This is done after the student has completed some non-music application homework. This final step helps cement the student's ability to use the skill comfortably and capably in wide-ranging applications. Those above-mentioned steps will easily fit into the traditional lesson format most music teachers are accustomed to using, especially if a little time is set aside in each meeting to do so. The **"Questions for Reflection"** section helps teachers take note of where their students were before using a particular skill and what benefits they may have gained after learning and applying a particular skill. **"Suggested Reading"** provides resources for both the teacher and the student to explore, regarding the chapter's particular skill topic. The **"References"** section is self-explanatory. And, finally, the **"Notes"** page is left blank for teachers to write observations or ideas they may have after reading and applying the chapter.

WHO WILL USE THIS BOOK?

This book is intended for both pre-college and college-level music teachers of *all* instruments and voice (even though my examples are largely piano-centric); there is also much potential for application in band and choral settings, and for study by college music students in pedagogy classes. There is a wide age range of application: basic skill concepts can be introduced as soon as the teacher feels a student can understand and assimilate them. As the student matures, these universal skills can be taught and applied in greater depth.

MUSIC OUTREACH AND ADVOCACY

The Transposed Musician makes a strong case for strengthening and supporting music education programs, offering messages that music educators can use strategically to advocate for their field. It presents an approach through which universal skills—the very ones legislators, business leaders, and school/university administrators unanimously agree are so critical—can be effectively taught through the study of music.

It is hoped that the ideas for universal skill learning and transposition presented in this book will become powerful catalysts upon which music educators can expand and develop new ideas and approaches. The ideas found here can also be used to create and support partnerships between researchers and practitioners by speaking to the very core of interdisciplinary thinking and the idea of universal skill application through transference. Not surprisingly, schools such as Stanford University and Davidson College are engaging initiatives that embrace partnerships between wide varieties of disciplines within their schools, with universal skills playing a significant connecting role. This reflects the increasing awareness that universal skill intersection between disciplines has great potential to provide new and useful insights.

Finally, I hope the ideas put forth in this book will give further support to music teachers to forge new and stronger relationships with legislators, administrators, community leaders, and business leaders. This could lead to greater support and funding for music in general and the creation of music programs that integrate teaching universal skills via the study of music. Nothing would please me more.

REFERENCES

1. College Music Society, "The End of the Conservatory." Pre-conference workshop. College Music Society 2016 National Conference, Santa Fe, NM, 10-26-2016.
2. Carolina/CMS Summit 2.0. "21st Century Music School Design" University of South Carolina, Columbia, SC. 1-17/20-2019.
3. Toppo, Greg. "Oberlin Eyes Enrollment Swap." Inside Higher Ed. https://www.insidehighered.com/news/2019/04/18/amid-budget-deficits-and-unfavorable-demographics-oberlin-pushes-do-more-less (accessed 12-19-2019).
4. Weirich, Robert. "Winds of Change." *Clavier* Magazine, July/August, 2018, vol. 10, No. 4.
5. Kaplinsky, Yoheved. "Most FAQ Regarding the Mechanics of Piano Playing." Conference Lecture, World Piano Pedagogy Conference, Anaheim, CA, 10-26-2005. (Aural recollection of the author.)
6. Pettit, Emma. "Columbia Had Little Success Placing English Ph.Ds. on the Tenure Track. 'Alarm' Followed, and the University Responded." Chronicle of Higher Education. https://www.chronicle.com/article/Columbia-Had-Little-Success/246989 (accessed 8-21-19).
7. Ibid.

CHAPTER I

PROBLEM-SOLVING

"We cannot solve our problems with the same level of thinking
that created them."
—Albert Einstein. [1]

"First, teachers must become crafters of problems. I think this is
the most important shift teachers can make…"

"Teachers must also make the shift to being process instructors in
addition to being content instructors."
—Ted McCain. [2]

"To recognize problems, musicians need keen perceptual skills."
—Gerald Klickstein. [3]

Problem: "a question raised for inquiry, consideration, or
solution…a source of perplexity, distress, or vexation." [4]

Solve: "to find a solution, explanation, or answer for a problem."[5]
—Merriam-Webster's Collegiate Dictionary

I. SKILL IMPORTANCE, CONTEXT, DEFINITION, AND BREAKDOWN

SKILL IMPORTANCE

Problem-solving is one of the best universal skills you can teach your student. Once learned, problem-solving can unlock almost any difficulty. Don't leave this process to chance, however, and expect that your music students will figure out on their own how to problem-solve with any depth or consistency. Instead, use a step-by-step process for them to gain the best results. Unfortunately, almost all my incoming freshmen demonstrate poor problem-solving skills; showing me how little previous instruction they have had with this skill. Fixing this deficit is one of my first priorities after they arrive.

SKILL CONTEXT

Problem-solving is not just a critical skill for the music studio; it is also one of the most sought-after skills in the workplace. Over and over we read statements from business leaders and CEOs that problem-solving skills are in short supply. In *Raising the Bar Survey*, by Hart Research Associates on behalf of the Association of American Colleges and Universities, 75% of all employers polled cited "the ability to analyze and solve complex problems" as one of the skills employees must have.[6] Your students will use this skill not only in the music practice room, but throughout all aspects of their lives and professions.

SKILL DEFINITION

Problem-solving, then, is a specific process for finding answers or solutions to something that is either not known or not fully known.

The process used to solve a problem can either be willy-nilly, as it often is, or systematic. We will explore the latter, a far more efficient and effective process.

As most of us know, musicians can't function very well without problem-solving skills. Music presents a myriad of problems for students to solve, spanning interpretive and technical issues. Yet, in spite of these challenges, in my many years of teaching, I have rarely met a music student who can articulate an effective problem-solving system or series of steps. It's clear that musicians could benefit from a little more training in problem-solving.

SKILL BREAKDOWN

PROBLEM SOLVING STEPS:

In my experience, these problem-solving steps work best.

1. Realize that a problem exists. (Not as easy as it may seem.)

2. Define the problem. (Locate, isolate, and determine what the issue actually is.)

3. Develop a plan of action. (What steps will be taken to resolve the problem spot? What resources may be needed, such as additional information or expert advice? Divide and conquer.)

4. Execute the plan of action and evaluate results. (Test the solution to see what worked and what did not.)

5. Trial and error. (Apply this step when no clear solution exists.)

6. Reconstruction. (Put the dissected section back together and into context and then repeat for security.)

II. TONIC KEY
Learn to Apply the Skill to Music

DESCRIPTION OF STEPS

1. REALIZE THAT A PROBLEM EXISTS

In this first step, the student must be able to determine that something is wrong so that they actually stop playing and try to figure out *what* the problem is. The importance of this essential first step to problem-solving can't be underestimated, for obvious reasons. Surprisingly, the issue of not knowing a problem exists—or exactly what the problem is—is more common than one might think and still prevalent at the college level. As Klickstein's quote at the beginning of this chapter knowingly states, this step is all about the student's level of perception. Not surprisingly, developing and elevating their ability to perceive is one of our most important jobs as teachers!

Since aural perception and retention is the key component for a musician in realizing a problem exists, how is that perception developed? Primarily, while practicing, the student must try to make sure that a part of their mind is always dedicated to the task of *perceiving* and *recalling* the sounds they are creating. It's like having a second pair of ears whose sole job is quality control. In the early stages, most students are preoccupied with the bewildering array of cognitive and physical demands involved in just getting notes to sound in some semblance of order; consequently, there is little-to-no capacity left to listen well and recall with much accuracy. With persistence (and much help from their teachers), however, students will begin to develop their perception skills. It's a long process.

Aural perception practice

Here are some practice tips to help develop aural perception skills:

a.   You play short sections of repertoire your student already knows, but include wrong notes or rhythms for the student to catch. Although the student is not playing in this exercise, they *are* learning to develop and trust their ear. Being able to pick out and recall multiple errors in a single example is a goal.

b.   Next, ask the *student* to play a section of music that has been problematic—ask them to listen as intently as they can while playing, to specifically identify what and where errors or challenges might be. It may be necessary to ask leading questions to help direct their attention to problem areas.

c.   Have your student listen to recorded music of top artists (the student's instrument at first), focusing upon one element at a time (rubato, articulation, singing line, or pedaling). To get started, listen with them and ask specific questions such as: how did the artist use rubato (liberally or sparingly); how many different articulations were used (staccato, legato, accents); what levels of dynamics did they hear; etc.? By having a student practice focusing on these various elements, one at a time, you help increase their sensitivity to each, increasing their ability to perceive. As in learning all things, take small steps at first. Encourage your students to listen to music in this way each day.

Once your student's aural perception ability increases, they will find that their practice efficiency improves. This is because they will be identifying errors more quickly and accurately and starting the process toward fixing them sooner and with more detail on what to do. Of course, good score-reading habits are extremely important in this equation. How does the student catch a wrong note or a missed slur in a passage, for example, if they have misread it in the score and/or never heard it correctly in the first place? They won't. Therefore, the student must take great care to read and mind the score.

2. DEFINE THE PROBLEM

Specifying and isolating the issue is next: is it a wrong note or rhythmic error or something else? Students, especially at the lower levels, often have difficulty ascertaining exactly what or where the problem actually is, even though they *are* aware, vaguely, that one exists (step one). They may say at this juncture, "It doesn't sound right, but I can't quite pinpoint the problem—so I'm not sure what to do next." This observation does not have to be a dead end. Because students need to learn how to determine the exact nature of *what* the problem is, it is of the utmost importance that they constantly work to improve their level of perception. Meanwhile, they must not forget to record themselves using their ever-present smartphone. This will make it easier to identify errors since they aren't engaged in the act of playing and can focus all their attention on listening. Encourage students to involve another (better) set of ears when possible.

Teachers play a big role here to help the student better pinpoint a problem. You may have to provide them with a basic diagnostic list of the usual suspects, such as: notes, articulation, rhythm, phrasing, dynamics, etc. Then, ask the students to check each one of those "suspects" separately by playing the section through multiple times in order to locate the culprit. Reminding them to carefully look at the score, while they are going through their sequence of checks, is a must.

3. DEVELOP A PLAN OF ACTION

Once the problem has been pinpointed, such as a difficult rhythm in a tricky technical passage, your student will need to decide what steps they will take to make the needed corrections. The most important technique at this stage is breaking a problem into manageable parts or sections—also known as divide and conquer. It is surprising to me how many students try to "eat the whole steak in one mouthful," so to speak, instead of many small, manageable bites. This is to say, when students get to a problem spot in their music, they often overburden themselves by trying to do too much at once. This would include: practicing too large a chunk of music; practicing more than one issue at a time (trying to fix rhythmic *and* technical issues simultaneously); or just playing the passage too fast for their current level. I give my students another example for this tendency: as a beginning juggler, you wouldn't try to toss four balls in the air at first, it would be too difficult. Instead, you would start with one ball and then, once comfortable with the first, add a second ball and so on. That's a helpful picture to use when introducing the divide and conquer concept.

4. EXECUTE THE PLAN OF ACTION AND EVALUATE RESULTS

Here, the student tries their plan of action. They practice one element at a time, one hand at a time (for pianists), slowly, and in short sections that will be pieced together later. As they do this, they try to discern what seems to be working and what isn't. Perhaps the student thought they could solve a rhythm issue by counting out loud while they played. Upon trying and realizing that their original plan wasn't working (because they couldn't count through the passage steadily or didn't know precisely where the counts fell in the music), their adjusted plan of action could include the addition of using a metronome and/or writing the counting numbers into the score to increase their rhythmic accuracy.

Example of practice steps in the plan of action: say the tricky rhythmic passage in question is a piano part with a fast, awkward ascending RH scale which immediately transitions into a series of broken descending octaves. First, separate the scale from the broken octaves. Determine the best scale fingering and group according to the meter. Write in the counting numbers in their exact places in the score for visual reinforcement. Next, practice cycling thumb crossovers (play back and forth 3, 1, 4, 1, 3, 1, 4, 1, etc.) in the scale to increase fluency and evenness. Practice playing the scale slowly while counting and being reinforced by a metronome. Reduce use of the metronome. Increase the scale speed slowly.

Once that section is being managed and under control, the student would work on the next problem of the section: defining the appropriate physical gesture(s) that transition the hand and fingers from the end of the scale to the broken octaves. It is usually at transition points between different patterns that problems occur. Here, the student must ask themselves: what has to happen from the last note of the scale to the first note of the broken octave? What does the hand have to do to navigate that distance efficiently and with minimal motion? Once those questions are answered (often through some trial and error), the student should practice the transition itself, which would include only two or three notes of the scale and two or three notes of the start of the broken octaves. For the greatest efficiency, practice the transition over and over in an unbroken cycle to maximize time use and always practice at a tempo that allows for total accuracy. Increase speed only as accuracy allows. Finally, once the transition section is solid, add more notes on either side to work the passage back into the overall context. This whole process must be first developed under the watchful eye and guidance of the teacher in the lesson. Once the student has used and practiced this step consistently for a while, they will become adept at the cycle of try, evaluate, adjust, and retry. By doing so, they will find that their practice results and efficiency dramatically improves.

5. TRIAL AND ERROR

In their book, *Evolutionary Epistemology, Rationality and the Sociology of Knowledge*, Radnitzky and Bartley say, "Trial and error is a fundamental method of solving problems."[7] Stubborn problems, of course, can resist valiant attempts at a solution. When a student confronts such a problem and is at a loss for what to do next, it is especially important that they apply trial and error as an effective tool for such situations. If some students feel averse to this sort of approach, help them understand how important the need for risk-taking is in the problem-solving process and how necessary it will be to them when they will encounter the inevitable stubborn problem.

For many of us, trial and error is practiced on a day-to-today basis; we're just not often aware of it as such. At a simple level, for example, if a door handle won't open with a twist in one direction, we try turning the other way. If that didn't work, twisting harder the initial way might be tried next. Ultimately, one direction and/or using more force than before produces the desired effect. How would the successful attempt have occurred unless a number of different, exploratory tries were taken first? Clearly, that process was trial and error being applied to solve a problem.

Because trial and error has such potential to reveal solutions, it must always be considered part of the problem-solving process. Contrary to common opinion, trial and error is not merely trying things blindly in a wholly scatter-shot approach and hoping for a miracle. It is most often about following *educated guesses or hunches* and experimenting with possible solutions while keeping track of results and casting about for further solutions. The world is full of amazing examples resulting from the trial and error process—such as Goodyear's discovery of how to vulcanize rubber for the automobile tire. It took him five years to stumble upon just the right mix of sulfur, rubber, and heat.[8]

TRIAL AND ERROR TOOLS

For students needing to become adept at employing trial and error, here's a simple process with a few steps. Let's say a student is struggling to develop an interpretation of a phrase in a piece. However, nothing sounds quite right to them and they feel like giving up. Instead...

A. **Try extremes.** This will help define parameters. For the section in question, have the student:
    1. Play it louder, then softer than they ever thought necessary.
        Have them reflect on what they heard. Did this process help clarify a choice for a particular dynamic?

2. Play it with an overabundance of rubato, then with none. Reflect. How might this step help reveal a clearer choice for the use of rubato in a particular section or piece?

3. Think like an actor; apply a different character to the section. For example: play it robustly, then meekly, overly expressive, then with no expression or character at all. Reflect. Often during this process the student will discover a new path of interpretation—perhaps something quite compelling.

B. **Mix and match.** When a student has difficulty figuring out or choosing which way an interpretation in a passage might go, they might learn something useful in trying to mix and match a variety of tempos, rubatos, dynamics, inflections, or articulations (with *some* relationship, of course, to the composer's directives). For example, suggest that your student keep track of the various combinations (use paper/pencil or voice recording) and then evaluate which combination seems best. What resulted when they tried an extreme dynamic with no rubato? What if they diminished the dynamic range and included some rubato at the same time? By mixing and matching in this way, students will not only discover solutions to interpretive problems; they will also improve their fluency with manipulating interpretive elements in their playing. Those possibilities will then lead to others and continue to help the student gain further confidence in using interpretive elements—all of which will help their level of musicianship.

C. **Get comfortable making errors.** For those students averse to making errors, counsel them to be especially open to what errors "tell" them, as William Westney explains in his book, *The Perfect Wrong Note*. "Honest mistakes are not only natural, they are immensely useful. Truthful and pure, full of specific information, they show us with immediate, elegant clarity where we are right now and what we need to do next."[9] Also, encourage students to be willing to follow hunches and what may seem like crazy possibilities—always while being perceptive—so they don't miss something that might be a significant technical or musical discovery.

D. **Select *a* solution when multiple ones seem like a toss-up or a choice is unsure.** Sometimes a student won't come to any solution (conclusion) because they are unsure of the choice(s) upon which they have decided. Or, perhaps two choices seem to work equally well. At this juncture, it is best to just pick *a* solution and go with it—time will tell whether the solution was the best choice or not. Changes can always be made later.

6. RECONSTRUCTION

The final step of the problem-solving process for the musician involves piecing elements back together. As each of the separated parts of the problem become manageable, students must slowly and carefully piece the sections back together, one by one, so that they integrate into the whole section or piece. It is important to remember not to try to put too much back together at once or play the reassembled parts too fast. Replication is necessary in all practice stages to ensure security. Patience! Alert the student to be on guard for the natural tendency to rush.

Practicing and piecing sections of the score back together is benefitted dramatically by creating a good aural "picture" of how the final product should sound (hearing it inside the head)—an aural picture must dictate the practice. How does a painter paint an image they can't bring to mind? The same idea holds true for the musician—how do you play or practice something that you can't yet hear internally? For most early-level students, developing an aural picture of a piece may be too advanced a practice without first starting them with some simple steps, such as audiating and singing out loud the dynamic contour of one phrase or one simple melody to start. As students improve, the audiation process can include larger sections of music, such as multiple phrases and elements including pitch, interval, harmony, etc. (Much more is said on the audiation process in Chapter Two, Focus.)

TENACITY

Churchill famously said, "Never, never, never give up." With that quote in mind, make sure your students understand the importance of tenacity in the problem-solving process. I mention this because many students wildly underestimate the time and resilience it takes for changes and improvements to solidify during the problem-solving process. Impress upon them that effort and will are elements for which there is no substitute. The big question is: how do students summon those elements forth, especially when they seem to be in short supply? Further, how does one try to instill will and effort in a student? It may not be enough just to mention to a student that it will take significant time and effort to work through an issue. Without tenacity and discipline to stay on task, the problem may not be solved well or at all. Here are some ideas to help.

DEVELOPING TENACITY

With students for whom tenacity seems to be a challenge, a teacher may help them develop this quality by being especially careful to give assignments which contain the right balance of challenge and reward (this may require some trial and error on the part of the teacher). In other words, give the student a challenge which requires effort, but not so much that they give up. When a student successfully meets a challenge, it is important to celebrate that moment with them (take time to recognize the accomplishment). Helping a student through a series of progressively harder cycles of challenges is one way to help them build tenacity. In essence, the student is building "tenacity endurance" and the recognition/reward component helps to keep them motivated to push a little further each week.

Helping a student discover and focus on the things they love about music is another way to help develop the tenacity needed to bring pieces of music to performance level. It certainly is easier to stick with something if it is pleasurable. Perhaps one of your students is especially attracted to playing music that contains significant quantities of lyricism. Helping them fully recognize that attraction might be a good first step. Then, helping them find lyricism in music where it is not so obvious would be another step in helping them expand their musical universe.

III. PIVOT CHORD
Prepare to Transpose the Skill to a Non-Music Application

Now let's prepare to apply (take) the steps for problem-solving in music to non-music areas. The steps are the same. Just as the pivot chord uses common pitches from one key to a new key, the common steps for problem-solving can also be transferred ("transposed") from a music application to a non-music application. The teacher "prepares" students for the transposition of the skill by reminding them of the music application steps and asking some (provided) questions that help students to discover the common ground in the new, non-music uses of the skill.

TRANSFERENCE—
THE IMPORTANCE OF APPLYING THE SKILL UNIVERSALLY

Each universal skill you help your students learn to apply to music in order to improve their playing can give them additional benefits when you help them learn to transfer the skill to other areas of their life. Continue to reinforce how they can benefit from using their universal skills for *any* application throughout the course of lessons you give them. As a reminder, this transference step will not take much time from the lesson and you don't need to be knowledgeable about subjects outside of music. You simply pose questions (suggested in each chapter) in a general way to help the student define the nature of a problem outside the field of music, enabling them to come closer to possible solutions. To teach problem-solving steps for a non-music application, you follow the same familiar outline you did in the music application.

Why include skill transference in the lesson? It's no secret that a big majority of our students do not become full-time professional musicians—including the legions of music students who go on to become doctors, scientists, teachers, etc. Since so many of the universal skills used in the process of learning music are equally important in non-music professions, making universal skill transference a significant aspect of the music lesson is a powerful addition to students' training. I believe that the music lesson is a uniquely-suited format to develop these universal skills. For the students who *are* going to make music their life's work, it is crucial to explain to them that practicing problem-solving (and other universal skills) in *non-music applications* will circle back to reinforce and strengthen their ability to apply the skill in music—thus benefiting their performance abilities. Using the same skill in multiple disciplines, known as transference, is a key aspect of this book. The following section shows you how transference can be incorporated into the lesson. (We know that a melody or section of music is more fully developed by transposing it to a new key area, so imagine how musicians become "transposed" after they learn to apply universal skills to all aspects of life, not just music).

IV. TRANSPOSITION
Actively Transpose the Skill to a Non-Music Application
NON-MUSIC APPLICATIONS

Once your student has become proficient in applying problem-solving steps in music, introduce the skill as something also highly applicable to non-music areas as well. You can start by asking your student to identify a problem area in a non-music setting—you will probably get quite a range of answers! Naturally, as teachers specializing in music, we are not going to be knowledgeable in all the problem areas that might come up. However, we can pose questions in a general way to help the student define the nature of the problem, enabling them to come closer to possible answers.

Some students may need a little more explanation to help them start thinking about a skill transference example. In this case, you might inquire if they are currently working on a challenge or problem in a class or project. Ask, "Would the same problem-solving steps you have learned to apply in your Bach fugue also work on the challenges in a project at school?" (I want to reiterate that no matter what the student may bring up in this section, you do not need to have or acquire any knowledge of it. To make this point abundantly clear, I have purposely created an example in which your student brings up chemistry as a place to apply their problem-solving skills. All you need to do is to ask a few questions in each of the same problem-solving steps, just as you have already covered in the music application above.)

I. RECOGNIZE THAT A PROBLEM EXISTS

In answer to your earlier question, perhaps your student Zenia brought up a problem she was experiencing in her chemistry class. (Wait, don't panic! As the music teacher, you need absolutely zero knowledge of chemistry to ask some leading questions. The following are exactly the same questions you used in the music application of problem-solving. Furthermore, it is not your job to know chemistry. Each chapter will give you more examples of how this transfer works.) Continuing with Zenia, you might reply, "Good, you have not only recognized that there *is* a problem to be solved in your chemistry class, but you also acknowledged it to yourself as well. That is an important, first step."

2. DEFINE THE PROBLEM

Here, you would ask Zenia, "What specifically doesn't seem to work in chemistry class?" She might reply that she did not have enough details or information to conduct an experiment. You ask, "Why is that? What seems to be at the root of your lack of information issue—is the teacher not clear or are you not paying enough attention? Or, are you not reading directives in the textbook carefully enough?" After thinking about it for a moment, Zenia replies that it is a little of both—not reading and following directives well enough in the textbook and not always paying attention in class. You would then ask her to develop a plan of action to solve those issues.

3. DEVELOP A PLAN OF ACTION

What Zenia does here must be directly related to her conclusions to the questions you posed in the previous step. In this example, she realized that she must make it her goal to better follow the directives in her textbook and pay more attention in class. She must now create a plan of action that will require her to gather information more carefully, whether in reading assignments or listening during lectures. For example, Zenia could write out a plan she creates outside of the piano lesson. What might her steps be? She could include her ideas on how she will try to stay more focused on her teacher's instructions and how she can better follow her textbook and pay attention in class.

4. EXECUTE THE PLAN OF ACTION AND EVALUATE RESULTS

This step requires Zenia to assess whether or not she has achieved the goals in her plan of action: i.e., was she able to successfully complete her chemistry lab experiments by getting the correct results?

Here, she must take pains to follow every step in the textbook to the letter to successfully complete her chemistry experiment (where perfectly measured material amounts, mixtures, and temperatures must be adhered to—just like carefully reading a score). By strictly adhering to the experiment protocol (as described in her textbook), Zenia realizes how sloppy her previous attempts had been.

The evaluation stage in this example would be Zenia determining whether or not her experiment outcome was what her textbook said it would be.

5. TRIAL AND ERROR

As mentioned earlier, trial and error is sometimes a necessary part of the problem-solving process—sometimes a plan of action is not clear and another approach is needed. Remember, trial and error need not be a scatter-shot approach; it should be a tactic based on educated hunches. This approach is used in most disciplines to some degree or another. In sports, for example, players often try small adjustments or variations to a tennis serve or a baseball pitch to see what works more effectively.

What if Zenia needed one more part of the puzzle to be able to successfully complete her chemistry experiment? What if she followed the textbook's directions as best she could and listened carefully in class, but still didn't get the desired results in her experiment? How might trial and error play a role? Here, you ask Zenia to think about which parts of the textbook's instructions she might safely be allowed to "adjust" in order to achieve a successful experiment. She can think about that on her own time outside the lesson. (Perhaps she was momentarily exceeding the temperature of a liquid during the heating process and not realizing that it was because she was turning the flame up too high--something trial and error could remedy.)

It is important to let Zenia know that no matter how clear a plan of action may be during the problem-solving process in any discipline, there may be the need to adjust just a bit to get the plan of action to work. Trial and error can benefit this necessary stage.

6. RECONSTRUCTION

In this step, the teacher makes sure to tell Zenia how important it is to put things all back together after focusing on one or two specific issues within a project. Here, you instruct her to make sure the solved issue works in the context of the whole project, just as in the music application, by replicating a successful action to see if the results remain the same. As in music, can the chemistry experiment be repeated successfully after working the first time? That is the ultimate goal in this final problem-solving step. She reports to you that this step is just like testing a tricky passage in a piece of music by playing it a number of times to see if it holds up consistently at tempo and in the context of the whole movement or piece. Experimentation and replication are part of the reconstruction process, regardless of the field.

V. RECAP
Revisit the Skill in Music

At this step, your students have practiced their problem-solving skills in both the music and non-music applications. They can now identify problem areas, pin-point issues, create and execute plans of action, evaluate results, employ trial and error, and finally, put things back together in the crucial and final step of reconstruction. Encourage them to use their new-found problem-solving tool whenever the need arises and to be consciously aware that they can always improve their problem-solving skill by thinking about the process and honing the sections they feel could use some additional work.

It is at this point that you direct your students' attention back to their problem-solving skill as it relates to music—something you have already covered well in past lessons. Ask them if using the skill *outside* the field of music provided them with any additional insights or ability to use it *in* the field of music. Encourage your students to reflect on the potential benefits of universal skill transference after they have applied them in various situations. For example: did following the chemistry experiment protocol to the letter provide Zenia with renewed conviction to do the same when following the dictates of a composer and her teacher (instead of carelessly ignoring some of them)? Did using trial and error in the chemistry lab provide a better perspective on using the same process in music? Did repeating the chemistry experiment (to make sure she could replicate the desired results) give her a new appreciation and zeal for taking the extra time and effort to increase the repetitions of those tricky passages to help make them more secure?

Those are the reasons for transference—all the possibilities for one application to help another. It is a cross-training procedure which more fully benefits and informs students in the use of a specific skill when it is applied in diverse situations and disciplines.

VI. QUESTIONS FOR REFLECTION

1. How has a comprehensive knowledge of problem-solving improved your students' practice and performance?

2. Would your students benefit from a master class focusing on problem-solving in music?

3. How might a lecture on problem-solving from someone *outside* the field of music, such as in a STEM field (science, technology, engineering, math), provide new insights for your music students' use of the skill?

4. Through transference, has your students' use of problem-solving in non-music areas further benefited their music practice?

5. Do your students see the problem-solving skill as something they can continually improve and use more comprehensively?

6. Are your students able to clearly teach back to you all the problem-solving steps you have taught them and demonstrate the process at their instrument?

VII. SUGGESTED READING

Adair, John. *Decision Making and Problem Solving.* Trowbridge, Wilshire, Great Britain: The Cromwell Press, 2003.

Jones, Morgan, D. *The Thinker's Toolkit: Fourteen Powerful Techniques for Problem-Solving.* New York City, NY: Three Rivers Press, 1998.

Levitt, Steven, D., and Stephen J. Dubner. *Think Like a Freak.* New York City, NY: William Morrow and Co., 2014.

Watanabe, Ken. *Problem-Solving 101: A Simple Book for Smart People.* New York City, NY: Penguin Books, 2009.

Zaccaro, Edward. *Becoming a Problem Solving Genius.* Bellevue, IA: Hickory Grove Press, 2006.

VIII. REFERENCES

1. Michael Armine, *Atomic Education Urged by Einstein* (New York Times, May 25, 1946, 13). (Common paraphrase of Einstein attributed to this article.)

2. Ted McCain, *Teaching for Tomorrow: Teaching Content and Problem-Solving Skills* (Thousand Oaks, CA: Corwin Press, 2005), 76.

3. Gerald Klickstein, *The Musician's Way: A Guide to Practice, Performance, and Wellness* (Oxford, UK: Oxford University Press, 2009), 55.

4. Merriam-Webster's Collegiate Dictionary, 10th ed. (1994), s.v. "problem."

5. Ibid., s.v. "solve."

6. Hart Research Associates, on behalf of the Association of American Colleges and Universities.

7. Gerald Radnitzky and William Bartely, *Evolutionary Epistemology, Rationality and the Sociology of Knowledge* (Chicago, IL: Open Court Publishing, Company, 1987), 94.

8. Christopher McFadden, "Charles Goodyear: The Father of Vulcanization," Interesting Engineering, accessed 12-16-2019, http://interestingengineering.com

9. William Westney, *The Perfect Wrong Note, Learning to Trust Your Musical Self* (Pompton Plains, NJ: Amadeus Press, 2003), 62.

IX. NOTES

CHAPTER 2

FOCUS

"Anything we can do to increase children's capacity for cognitive
control will help them throughout life."
—Daniel Goleman.[1]

"In every moment of your life, your skills are growing. The
question is, in what direction?"
—Thomas M. Sterner.[2]

"It's almost impossible to accomplish anything significant
when you are racing through an endless litany of tasks and
emergencies."
—Michael Hyatt.[3]

I. SKILL IMPORTANCE, CONTEXT, DEFINITION, AND BREAKDOWN

SKILL IMPORTANCE AND CONTEXT

Focus is an invaluable skill. With it, you can move mountains. When I talk to musicians and non-musicians, most agree that focus is *the* most critical component of high-level performance in any discipline. How often have we heard that it was superior focus which allowed one person to succeed where another equally prepared or equally talented person failed? Winning sports teams and athletes speak of mental tenacity and "being in the zone," surgeons speak of the hours spent in a difficult operation in which a moment's loss of concentration could prove injurious or fatal to the patient, and chess champions have been known to focus so intensely during match play that they lose weight. Professional musicians also focus with laser-like intensity for hours at a time during rehearsal or performance. As important as focus is while practicing, it is perhaps even more critical during performance, when the pressure is on and the stakes are high. In such situations, focus can be one of the most dauntingly difficult skills to master. Without consistent and significant focus, high-level practice and performance is simply not possible. If focus wanders, the music suffers.

In my experience as a performing pianist, focus is the most important skill by far. It has also been the most difficult skill to develop and maintain. It should not be surprising that while intense and sustained focus is not only the most difficult skill for music students to acquire, it is also the one they need the most. Lack of focus affects every aspect of their playing, from inefficient practice to spotty lessons to poor performances. Over the decades, most of my incoming piano students have consistently assured me they know how to focus. In reality, they exhibit a profound lack of focus skills; I have witnessed far too many student musicians struggle to maintain focus for even short periods of time. As a result, I spend a considerable amount of time helping my students learn to focus well. Many of my new students mistakenly equate the amount of time spent in the practice room to successful practice time—as if they were substituting "time" for "focus." However, as psychologist and focus expert Daniel Goleman says, "Hours and hours of practice are necessary for great performance, but not sufficient. How experts in any domain pay attention while practicing makes a crucial difference."[4] To say it another way: experts must focus intensely to get the superb results they do. Mental focus is the opposite of mental wandering—where the mind goes off topic and chatter dominates.

For musicians who must memorize, focus is an all-important component. Focus and memory are closely-linked and both have similar results when they are not functioning well: frequent glitches, slow progress, poorly-learned music, and over-all inconsistent performance. Here is how you can tell the difference between a student's lack of focus and lack of memorization: if memory is the issue (the data simply isn't there because of poor, spotty preparation), then the same place in the piece will always fail in repeated play-throughs. However, if poor focus is the issue, then *different* parts of the same piece will have glitches on repeated play-throughs. No matter how well a piece of music might be learned and memorized, without focus, its delivery will suffer.

SKILL DEFINITION

What is focus? Why is it so hard to master? How do you develop it? Dictionaries define focus using terms of convergence: a place where multiple lines intersect. In other words, all attention converges on one thing—just as light beams pass through a magnifying glass to form a highly condensed point of light and heat. To focus the mind, all attention must be similarly aimed. A deeper, more comprehensive understanding of focus can be found in the work of psychologist Mihályi Csikszentmihályi, who coined the word "flow" to describe the highly focused, single-minded mental state where "Concentration is so intense that there is no attention left over to think about anything else." [5] Similarly, Timothy Gallwey described this state as "getting in the zone"[6] in reference to high-level athletic performance. Eckhart Tolle speaks to the power of being in the present by saying "Realize deeply that the present moment is all you have. Make the Now the primary focus of your life."[7] At the root of each of those descriptions of focus lies the centuries-old practice of meditation. The origin of the word "meditation" comes from the Latin verb, *meditari*—to contemplate. The basic goal in meditation is to focus on one single thing for a period of time—also known as a state of mindfulness.

Many types of meditation require that we take our focus off our thoughts and place our focus or awareness on our breath. Indeed, it is upon the breath where we will start our focus practice. Later, once the student has learned to focus on the breath, they will be asked to transfer that single-mindedness to playing their instrument. It is important to point out that focus in music (and in other disciplines) requires that the mind overlooks everything except that which needs all our attention at that moment, such as playing a series of chords, swinging a bat, or moving a chess piece. It is important to note that overlooking distractions is different from *eliminating* distractions. Distractions can't always be eliminated, but you can become an expert at overlooking them; some call it looking through them. Being in the present moment and staying in the moment is very much a part of focus. Performance enhancement specialist Don Greene offers this insight on focus: *"Presence*—how to stay in the moment, and not leap ahead or drift into the past."[8]

Think of the mind as a muscle: the strength of focus can be increased just as a weightlifter builds muscle: through repetition. Increasing the duration and intensity in workouts increases the size of a muscle; increasing the duration and intensity of meditating literally increases the *size* of a portion of the brain associated with focus. A scientific study concluded that "meditation experience is associated with increased cortical thickness."[9] We can actually see this: with mindfulness meditation, "MRI scans show...the prefrontal cortex— associated with higher order brain functions such as awareness, concentration and decision-making, becomes thicker."[10] Therefore, the practice of focus can actually have physical, tangible results upon the brain.

SKILL BREAKDOWN

I believe a major reason so many music students struggle with focus is because it is not commonly taught as a *process*. It very surely is a process, however, and one that can include exercises with a series of steps to be practiced and assessed: stuff that is specific and tangible. To focus, the mind needs a specific object of attention. In music, the object(s) of attention must be *tangible elements*, such as recalling tonal centers, harmonies, intervals, sequences, patterns, keys, or noticing physical sensations in rhythm, embouchure, muscle support, kinetic motion, awareness of breath intensity, etc. Later, through much practice, all of those elements blend into one composite whole in the mind and become reflexive—you think it, it happens. The sole purpose of all of this is to allow one to form a specific sound at a specific moment on their instrument easily—this, to me, amounts to the afore-mentioned idea of flow or being in the zone. To begin the path of achieving this, we must help our students start to continually monitor their focus: if attention lapses, they must redirect the mind back to one of those pre-selected objects.

This tactic of redirection matches Goleman's cognitive cycle of focus during meditation: "the mind wanders, you notice it's wandering, you shift your attention to your breath, and you keep it there."[11] For musicians, that same cycle must happen during practice and performance and is a key concept I introduce to my freshmen students. I have created six focus steps for use in the music lesson and for transference into other applications: focus on breath; set a goal-oriented regimen; transfer focus from breath to music; practice focus in music application; work to improve focus ability; and assiduously avoid mindless repetition. These steps will now be applied to music in the following section.

II. TONIC KEY
Learn to Apply the Skill to Music

APPLICATION OF SIX FOCUS STEPS

STEP ONE: FOCUS ON THE BREATH

To begin, introduce your students to the age-old basic meditative practice of sitting still in a quiet place and simply being aware of their breathing—becoming conscious of regular inhalation and exhalation. Focusing on breath helps the student start to get a sense of the process of holding the mind in place with a singular intent.

At first, a student may be able to focus on their breathing for only short periods—perhaps just a few seconds—before their mind wanders. No matter where a student's baseline focus ability begins, ask them to try to extend the duration of their focus, even if it is just a few consecutive seconds at a time. Learning to maintain focus requires daily incremental work—a habit that very much should be developed and tied to a student's daily practice regimen at their instrument.

STEP TWO: SET A GOAL-ORIENTED REGIMEN

Remind students to always set goals and to make them achievable. Daily goals with a smidgen of challenge are best, not ones that can't be met. To get started in setting goals for practicing focus, I have listed a few below.

Exercise: Timing the Focus Sessions
Start by asking your student to practice their focus session for just three to five minutes each day using a smartphone alarm to time

the session. This helps them avoid checking the time or allowing thoughts about the passage of time to interfere. During this timed period, the student should try repeatedly to sustain their focus on breath for as long as they can. It may be only ten to fifteen seconds at a time without a single thought intruding. No matter, if a thought intrudes, try again. To improve, set an obtainable objective, such as achieving thirty to forty-five seconds of sustained mental focus on breath, without substantial lapses, for the first couple of weeks. Prepare your students for the fact that developing sustained focus will be challenging and not easy—daily practice will be required for improvement. Students should work toward these goals:

- Maintaining an initial three-to-five-minute practice period each day dedicated to focus. Extend the time period as ability increases. This regimen must be addressed with the same intent and dedication as the student uses to practice the actual music.
- Starting the simple meditation exercise at the beginning of the day, *before* starting music practice. This will aid the practice session dramatically, because the mind has been quieted and prepared via focus.
- Perseverance: nothing much of value can be accomplished without adhering to goals and regular practice. The environment must be conducive (quiet) and the effort intense and sustained.

STEP THREE: TRANSFER FOCUS FROM BREATH TO MUSIC

Once your student's focus on the breath improves and can be singularly maintained for a minute or longer, it's time to transfer their focus practice from breath to music. This stage requires, among other things, that the student must be able to hear music "play" in their head. This process is also known as inner hearing—something almost everyone can do to some degree. Later, as the student is able to recall longer, more complex melodies, introduce them to a more involved inner hearing process known as audiation—a term coined by the well-known music learning theorist, Edwin Gordon. Audiation includes not only being able to hear a melody internally (in one's head), but being able to *identify* all the elements of what's being heard along the way, such as pitches, intervals, rhythms, and harmonies. Eventually, through significant practice and time, this advanced musical ability will allow the student to hear a whole recital program with most or all of those elements present, in an unbroken flow, in their head. That stage should be the student's ultimate focus goal. As I remind my students, having the ability to audiate well is integral to becoming a complete musician. Once all the details of the piece of music are clearly known (through audiation), students can perform with supreme confidence and the freedom to dwell fully in the expressive realm while playing. Here are three exercises to help students start their inner hearing practice.

Exercise: Introduce the Process of Focusing Solely on Sound
Knowing exactly what to focus upon and what to overlook is paramount. For the beginner, audiation won't be possible if all elements are attempted at once. Practice hearing them separately in a step-by-step manner to help reduce the complexity demands. At first, ask students (regardless of level) to hear only a melody in their head, such as the opening bars of "Twinkle, Twinkle, Little Star," "Happy Birthday," or "Mary Had a Little Lamb." I've never had

a student say they can't call to mind at least part of one of these familiar melodies. This first step clarifies the start of the process for them and helps them imagine what they will need to do later, on a larger scale, when they learn to include more elements of the inner hearing process and graduate to longer, more complex pieces.

Now, ask your student to sing the same melody out loud. This can give you a good sense of what they are actually hearing in their inner ear. As soon as your student becomes comfortable with hearing simple, short melodies internally, challenge them to try more difficult and longer ones, perhaps such as those found in pieces they are currently playing. Ask them to sing these melodies out loud as well (even if in part). Sometimes a student may be able to approximate only the contour of a melody as a start. If this stage is even more problematic, chances are the melody is not clear in their inner ear. (A few basics in breath support and tone may help here, too—sometimes, a student can't produce enough of a singing sound to allow their teacher to recognize a melody.) As always, keep goals achievable—in this case, choose another, simpler melody. The internal hearing practice will substantially increase students' ability to focus and at the same time, build stronger, necessary music skills.

As students continue to improve their audiation ability—think in months and even years—challenge them to start identifying specific pitches, intervals, and rhythms within a simple melody (but only one element at a time). Audiation requires that your students have some basic theory and aural skills knowledge. Remember, this is a skill for the more advanced or precocious student.

Exercise: Begin Audiation with Intervals

For this next stage, have students hear a melody (or a portion of one), such as "The Star-Spangled Banner," in their inner ear. This time, however, students must include naming the intervals out loud, using inner hearing as a guide. If that is problematic, at the very least, have them try to identify whether the intervals move either up or down and by step or leap. If the student were to name the actual intervals in the *Star-Spangled Banner,* they would articulate out loud: down m3, down M3, up M3, up m3, up P4, and so on. At first, the student may need to sing or play some intervals as they go, such as using a solfege system of fixed- or moveable-do, to help with accuracy. Then, ask them to identify the rhythms: in this case, dotted eighth, sixteenth, quarter, quarter, quarter, half, etc. If your student is a pianist, identifying harmony must be added to the mix as well— perhaps not every chord, but certainly primary chords, key centers, and some modulations.

For many students, audiation will be quite demanding and their minds may soon wander, tire, or balk at the amount of sustained focus required—that's a major reason why meditation is similarly so challenging. Keep the audiation exercise fairly short in the lesson (at least at first), but remind students to continue to practice it on their own throughout the week. Pushing your students a bit to persevere may be necessary.

Exercise: Audiation Assessment

As your students improve and move to audiating longer, more complex pieces (including harmonies for keyboardists), you will want to track their progress. The obvious question, of course, is just *how* do you know if your students are accurately hearing a piece unfold in their heads? To "step into" a student's mind and check their progress, pick a piece they know well and set a metronome to silent blink mode at a tempo you both agree upon. Then ask the student to start audiating the piece from memory at the pace of the metronome, while you follow along in the score. The metronome keeps you both in the same place at the same time. At various points along the way, say "stop" and ask the student to pinpoint exactly where they are in the piece. Students must demonstrate their location by humming the melody at the point where they were stopped, pointing to the place in the score, or playing the measure where they were stopped. The place should match exactly, or within a measure, of where you stopped them in the score. Of course, music is normally not metronomic and must breathe, but for this exercise, follow the metronome.

If the stopping places do not match, then the student may have let their mind wander, gotten behind, jumped ahead, or become lost. If that happens, ask them to try again. If the goal of arriving at the same place in the score consistently eludes the student, choose a simpler or shorter piece. This checking step will allow you to ascertain just how accurate your students' inner hearing and focus have become and improve your ability to help them through this process.

Here's a variation of the above exercise for music that doesn't work well with a metronome because of the necessary rubato or pauses. Ask your student to tap out their beats on the piano lid or table while they audiate—just ask which basic pulse they are tapping to (quarter, half note, etc.). In this way, the natural ebb and flow of a tempo can occur, yet still allow you to follow along in the score. As with the above exercise, the student must sing or play the measure where they were stopped. This will let you know that they were truly audiating and not just counting.

Doing these exercises will give an accurate indication of how solid your student's focus is—especially over longer sections and whole pieces. More work will be required of pianists in this focus exercise as layers of harmony and rhythm are added to the inner hearing process.

STEP FOUR: PRACTICE.

Focus is a mental muscle, strengthened by daily workouts. Because the mind often resists a strict regimen of control, it will naturally tend to wander when it is needed most, such as in practicing and performing. Remind your student that when they find their mind wandering, bring it back to what Goleman calls a "point of focus"[12] and continue. If the mind wanders again, they must gently nudge it back on track and continue. This process must be repeated over and over.

Students should understand that they must strive to increase the length and intensity of their focus incrementally—not expect it to improve in leaps and bounds. Their goal is to be able to control their focus for an entire piece and, ultimately, an entire program.

Exercise: "Switch on" Focus
As students improve their focus acumen, they can learn to "switch on" their focus as needed. This is exactly what must be done before walking out on stage and beginning to play. Gaining the ability to focus at will is something that will also have to be learned—this is in contrast to taking time to work into it. To practice getting to the point of "switching on" their focus at will, try this: have your students read a paragraph in a book or converse for a minute or two.

Then, suddenly have them stop and switch gears to focus on a piece they are about to play by asking them to walk to their instrument and begin. This sequence must be practiced to become dependable.

Remind your student that the mind, like a muscle, also needs periodic rest—intense focus can't be sustained endlessly. Practicing intensely for 30 to 40 minutes before taking a break is plenty. Rest breaks should last 5 to 10 minutes and, preferably, can involve some walking, stretching, and chatting in person (preferably not on social media) with friends. Your students will be amazed at how much more they will be able to accomplish in their practice sessions by maintaining a schedule of consistent, short rest breaks. This is akin to what athletes call interval training. More can be found on that topic in my chapter, Biomechanics and Physiology, in the book *A Symposium for Pianists and Teachers: Strategies to Develop the Mind and Body for Optimal Performance.*[13]

STEP FIVE: EVALUATE FOCUS ABILITY.

Here are some questions to ask your students to better evaluate their progress:
- How is your focus working?
- Can it be sustained through a performance?
- If it fails, when and where does it fail?
- What do you think can be done to improve it further?

Those questions can only be answered fully if your student views their focus practice regimen as an important part of their daily work, discusses it regularly with you, and notates their progress in a journal in order to keep track. For example, if a student's unbroken focus time increases from one to two minutes over a specific time interval, the student and teacher have a good sense of what sort of progress is being made. This evaluative aspect gives students a better sense of how close they are to goals and whether more work—and what kind—is necessary. This awareness of progress can really help propel a student forward, motivating them to continue.

STEP SIX: AVOID MINDLESS REPETITION

Although repetition is certainly a key ingredient in all practice—even while practicing audiation—many students may naturally fall into a kind of repetitive practice that is more mindless than mindful. Since my college days, I have heard countless students in practice rooms endlessly repeating problem spots with the hope they will "stick." Students flail in this way often for the lack of a better system, such as formulating the desired sound first in the mind (audiation) before physically trying to render it. Repetition of kinesthetic patterns without specific cognitive directives (such as what, specifically, will be done differently in the next repetition) is not an efficient use of practice time. Mindless repetition does not breed focus nor produce reliable results later, especially under the pressure of a lesson or a performance. Mindless practice allows the mind to wander, is very unproductive, and is the opposite of a focused, mindful approach.

III. PIVOT CHORD
Prepare to Transpose the Skill to a Non-Music Application

Once your student understands focus at a deeper level and has become somewhat proficient at it through practice, it is time to help them transfer this ability to a non-music area. Remember, you can help your students transfer each one of the universal skills presented in this book into a non-music application. You do not need any background knowledge in the non-music application that the student selects. The steps are the same. Think of the steps as the common tones in a pivot chord between two different key areas.

The transference process is a win-win proposition for the student: by transferring a skill, they learn to apply it to *any* aspect of life. I have found that using a universal skill outside the original music application can provide more insights into the skill itself—which then can circle back and benefit the music application still more. Here are a few questions to get your students thinking about transferring their hard-won focus skills to non-music applications.

Start by asking your students what subject or project outside their lesson could benefit from improved focus skills. For example, ask, "Do you have any difficulties staying on task or remaining focused when you work on a school project, a job, or when you try to learn something new? Does your mind wander, do you get distracted easily, or are you quickly thrown off your game?" If the answer is yes to any of those questions, follow up with some of the questions listed immediately below. You will notice that the questions you are posing to your students are equally applicable to the music and non-music applications.

1. HAVE YOU (THE STUDENT) TRIED NOTICING YOUR BREATH BEFORE YOU START YOUR NON-MUSIC TASK?

As the student first learned through the meditation exercise near the beginning of this chapter, an effective way to counter the mind's natural tendency to wander and help empty it of all things unimportant to the task at hand was to start focusing solely on the breath. This would help start them toward their ultimate goal of being able to better manage their mind by keeping it highly focused under pressure— such as during a performance. In such a situation, for example, a pianist can't be worrying about the difficult octave section on the next page, even when the mind strains to do so. Instead, they need to remain entirely in the moment, focusing only on right now.

Since your student first started their focus exercise by concentrating solely on the breath, it is also a good place for them to start before a *non*-music application...it can help trigger the "focus response." To do so, they can start by thinking (again) about their breath: is it shallow or deep, is it regular or irregular, is the mind often wandering off track? Once they feel their mind has come into focus, move to step two, below.

2. DO YOU EVER TRY THESE FOCUS DIAGNOSTICS WHILE DOING YOUR NON-MUSIC TASK?

- What, exactly, do you need to focus on? Be specific: i.e., solving a difficult math problem or listening carefully.
- What do you need to ignore or overlook? Be specific: i.e., a barking dog or a cell phone conversation.

- Which part of the music application for focus could help you the most here?
- Can you apply or adapt that same music exercise to this non-music task? How?

3. ARE YOU SETTING GOALS THAT REMIND YOU TO ENGAGE THE FOCUS PROCESS?

- Can you invent a plan to remember to focus on breathing, during the non-music event, or whenever you need it? (This will help initiate the focus process.)
- Can you think of a physical cue to use as a reminder to focus on breathing? Could you wear something, glance at something, or hold something (such as a wristband, a hand-written note, or a coin), to remind you to breathe or to reset your attention every time you notice the item?

If students don't do this step, they can easily fall into an old habit of embarking on an important task in an unfocused state, yielding less-than-optimum results.

4. CAN YOU VISUALIZE THE ENTIRE SEQUENCE OF A NON-MUSIC TASK?

Like audiation, visualization can be used as a practice run-through prior to the actual event. Visualization can include going through every aspect of a talk including the text, physical actions, interaction of the two, etc.

- Can you try to see yourself doing your non-music task in your mind's eye and being successful?
- What are the steps needed to complete that task and the problems that may be faced along the way?
- Can you imagine how you will feel after successfully completing the task?
- Will you make sure to try this visualization just before you begin your non-music task?
- How will you remember to do this?

5. DO YOU EVALUATE YOUR RESULTS?

Students need to know that the process of self-evaluation is as important to improving their focus abilities in non-music applications as it is in music. That process will help them to recognize where progress has been made and where it hasn't. They can start by asking themselves questions such as:

- How often did your focus wander? Why? Were you not vigilant enough?
- What specifically may have distracted you in a particular situation? What thing(s) or people or negative thoughts should you be ignoring or overlooking?
- How can you make adjustments to improve your focus? Is more discipline or practice needed to extend your periods of focus?

6. DO YOU PRACTICE MINDLESS REPETITION?

Ask your students:

- Do you notice that you tend to repeat non-music tasks without thinking about how they might be improved?
- What might you do to change that habit?
- Would there be any positive changes in your life if you were able to consistently focus fully on important tasks as they arise?
- Do you routinely 'allow' your mind to wander while you are doing important tasks that you know really require all of your attention?
- If so, how often does your mind wander? How can you reduce the number of instances?

IV. TRANSPOSITION
Actively Transpose the Skill to a Non-Music Application

By using just a few of the questions listed above, you help your piano student, Beth, to transpose (transfer) her new-found skills in focus to a non-music application. For example, you might ask her "Do you have a challenging class, or a project, or a job where you wish you had better focus?" She tells you that she wants to focus better in her debate team matches. She says she often gets sidetracked by the opponent in the midst of an intense debate. You ask, "Why do you get sidetracked?" (Please remember, as the music teacher, you don't need to know anything about debating skills.) Beth says it's because of the way some opponents get so hopped-up during the event. "I get distracted by the intensity of the other person when they are in competition." She feels her content and delivery suffer as a result. You ask, "What is it *specifically* that you want to ignore and what is it *specifically* you want to focus upon?" (These are exactly the same questions you have used to help her improve her focus on her music.) Beth replies, "I wish I could just focus on the words of the opponent and ignore the loudness or the aggressiveness in them." You ask, "What focus exercise in music helped you the most?" "Well, I think it's the one where I had to audiate the melody in my piano sonata. It's hard to think of anything else when you are naming every interval in a melody." "Good!" you reply. Now, you (the teacher), simply help her imagine how to transfer that same music focus exercise into a debate focus exercise. However, as mentioned above, it is not your job to know about debate skills—let Beth do that work—you are her "skill transposition coach," not her debate coach. You continue by saying "Beth, can you think of a way that naming intervals in a melody could be similar to focusing on your opponent's words and not his emotions?" Notice you are using her favorite focus exercise and asking her to use her imagination on how that could work in her self-described debate situation. "Yes," she replied, "I can see how the words of the opponent are the same as the notes in a melody—I'm supposed to focus on just that one thing. I'll try to start thinking about only the *meaning* of the words and ignore all the facial expressions and gesturing. You reply, "That sounds just like when you focus on the melody and ignore the intruding thoughts." Beth says, "Yes! I'll ignore his obnoxiousness by focusing on the words, the same way I try to ignore intruding thoughts when I am audiating a melody."

If Beth can't come up with an idea for how she would transfer the music focus exercise to her debate focus exercise during the lesson, it can become an assignment for the following week. Remember, as the teacher, you provide the thought-provoking questions; the students must find the connections.

V. RECAP
Revisit the Skill in Music

THE KEY TO FOCUS: HABITUALLY REMAIN IN THE PRESENT

When revisiting focus skills as they apply to music, remind your student to pull their mind back to the present whenever it drifts. They can do this by using audiation, or some component of it, as the primary target of their focus. Remaining in the present moment is the essential task in building their focus acumen. After my students are well-versed in these steps but their attention occasionally flags, I can easily remind them to get back on track with a simple, but now more meaningful, keyword: "focus." Habitually resetting their focus is a process that can become commonplace for them—but it has to be practiced consistently. Once the student has begun to learn to stay in the moment for any length of time, their focus ability has already been sharpened. Then, they will be able to react and function much more effectively to the needs of any given situation. As their teacher, be patient and continue to ask students to consistently practice their focus over the ensuing months and years.

You should ask your student: what new thoughts or insights, if any, came from using the skill in the non-music application? This question may not produce any response at first, but it is important to start the student thinking about how using a skill in one application can help inform its use in another application. However, perhaps Beth, in our example above, found that applying focus skills (first used in music) in her debate matches actually further strengthened her ability to focus during her piano performances because of the challenging kinds of distractions in that setting. That's an example of how a transferred skill "circles back" to further improve its original application.

EFFECTIVE SCORE STUDY VIA ADVANCED FOCUS SKILLS

As your students' focus becomes more sustained and powerful, it can be applied to more advanced uses such as learning and memorizing music *away* from the instrument, just by studying the score. As quizzical as your students might be upon hearing this statement, I can say without doubt, they can learn to do this! Begin with very easy pieces, then graduate to more difficult, lengthier pieces, as skill allows. I have often demonstrated this possibility to my students in piano class with a little in-class assignment. I ask them to learn and memorize a short, easy piece using only the score. My selection, usually homophonic, is about three lines long. After ten quiet minutes, I ask each of them to go to the piano and play it for the class from memory. On many occasions, students have been able to play the piece all the way through with no or almost no issues. Other students demonstrate a good grasp of the idea, even if they don't quite make it all the way through. I then surprise them by asking them to transpose the piece—something they have also shown they can do after trying. This seemingly impossible task became possible— right in front of their eyes and their classmates'! They were able to make this leap precisely because, by studying a piece away from the piano, they were forced to know the piece cognitively (theoretically) and aurally and *not* rely on the merely kinesthetic (physical) memory gained through repetitions. Relying solely on kinesthetic memory, we all know, is shaky at best; often breaking down under the least amount of pressure...unless, of course, it is reinforced by the critical cognitive and aural work just described. *That* is where security comes from in performance. It will do much to eliminate the common refrain we have all heard so often, "Well, I could play it through perfectly in the practice room!" Speaking to the idea of *really* knowing what you are playing, my piano professor at Indiana University had a wonderful saying, "What the mind knows, the hands will play."[14] It was, and is, so true.

Memorizing and practicing away from the instrument requires high-level focus skills—the holy grail of focus for experienced musicians. With time and patience, the student will recognize that solid focus skills will be one of their greatest abilities, one of their most powerful tools, and the key to doing *anything* well.

VI. QUESTIONS FOR REFLECTION

1. Did the exercise of focusing only on the breath help your students begin to rid their minds of chatter?
2. How has working on focus helped your students' score study and memorization?
3. Have they been able to play a piece or section of a piece without losing their train of thought?
4. Have these focus exercises helped your students in their non-music areas of study such as school and homework?
5. Has using focus in non-music applications helped your students to further solidify their focus ability in music?

VII. SUGGESTED READING

Csíkszentmihályi, Mihály. *Flow: The Psychology of Optimal Experience.* New York, NY: HarperCollins, 1990.

Gallwey, Timothy W. *The Inner Game of Tennis: The Classic Guide to the Mental Side of Peak Performance.* New York, NY: Random House, 1974.

Green, Don. *Fight Your Fear and Win: Seven Skills for Performing Your Best Under Pressure—at Work, in Sports, on Stage.* New York, NY: Broadway Books, 2001.

Goleman, Daniel. *Focus: The Hidden Driver of Excellence.* New York, NY: HarperCollins, 2013.

Gordon, Edwin. *Learning Sequences in Music: A Contemporary Learning Theory.* Chicago, IL: GIA Publications, Inc., 2007.

Ireland, Tom. "What Does Mindfulness Meditation Do to Your Brain?" *Scientific American Online*, 6-12-2014, https://blogs.scientificamerican.com/guest-blog/what-does-mindfulness-meditation-do-to-your-brain/.

Shockley, Rebecca. *Mapping Music: For Faster Learning and Secure Memory.* Middleton, WI: A-R Editions, 1997.

Tolle, Eckhart. *The Power of Now.* Novato, CA: New World Library *and* Vancouver, B.C., Canada Namaste Publishing, 1999.

VIII. REFERENCES

1. Daniel Goleman, Focus: *The Hidden Driver of Excellence* (New York, NY: HarperCollins, 2013), 81.

2. Thomas M. Sterner, *The Practicing Mind: Developing Focus and Discipline in Your Life* (Novato, CA: New World Library, 2005), 133.

3. Michael Hyatt, *Free to Focus: A Total Productivity System to Achieve More by Doing Less* (Grand Rapids, MI: Baker Books, 2019), 13.

4. Daniel Goleman, *Focus: The Hidden Driver of Excellence* (New York, NY: HarperCollins, 2013), 163-4.

5. Mihály Csíkszentmihályi, *Flow: The Psychology of Optimal Experience* (New York, NY: HarperCollins, 1990), 71.

6. Timothy W Gallwey, *The Inner Game of Tennis: The Classic Guide to the Mental Side of Peak Performance* (New York, NY: Random House, 1974), 14.

7. Eckhart Tolle, *The Power of Now* (Novato, CA: New World Library *and* Vancouver, B.C., Canada Namaste Publishing, 1999), 35.

8. Don Greene, *Fight Your Fear and Win: Seven Skills for Performing Your Best Under Pressure—at Work, in Sports, on Stage* (New York, NY: Broadway Books, 2001), 122-3.

9. Sara W. Lazar, et al, "Meditation experience is associated with increased cortical thickness" PubMed Online, 2-6-2006, www.ncbi.nlm.nih.gov/pmc/articles/PMC/1361002/ (accessed 5-25-17)

10. Tom Ireland, "What Does Mindfulness Meditation Do to Your Brain?" Scientific American Online (6-12-2014), https://blogs.scientificamerican.com/guest-blog/what-does-mindfulness-meditation-do-to-your-brain/ (accessed 6-12-17)

11. Daniel Goleman, *Focus: The Hidden Driver of Excellence* (New York, NY: HarperCollins, 2013), 168.

12. Ibid, 163-4.

13. Dylan Savage, et al, *A Symposium for Pianists and Teachers: Strategies to Develop the Mind and Body for Optimal Performance* (Dayton, OH: Heritage Music Press, 2002), 15.

14. Michel Block, piano faculty, Indiana University. From the author's recollection of multiple lessons at Indiana University, 1988-92.

IX. NOTES

CHAPTER 3

PATIENCE

"Never before has patience been more needed—and never has it been in such short supply."
—M. J. Ryan.[1]

"The wonderful thing about patience, unlike time, is the more we use it, the more we have."
— Alan Lokos.[2]

"It's not that I am so smart, it's just that I stay with problems longer."
—Albert Einstein.[3]

I. SKILL IMPORTANCE, CONTEXT, DEFINITION, AND BREAKDOWN

SKILL IMPORTANCE

How many students rush the process of learning a new piece? How often do students, in their hurry to finish a piece, short-change details in the music and allow incorrect habits to gain a foothold? Ironically, in their youthful enthusiasm to learn pieces as quickly as possible, students often end up taking much longer to finish a piece because of the time needed to undo mistakes and ill-gained habits. How thoroughly and much more quickly would students learn to finish a piece if they exercised the patience to fully absorb the details in the score? The propensity to rush through a piece to the detriment of detail is not solely the domain of younger students; I see this tendency in older students too. The tortoise and hare fable must always be re-told in the music lesson!

Although patience has long been called a virtue, I will refer to it here as a universal skill in the context of the music lesson. It's not an easy skill to master—and understandably so, especially now in our "age of immediacy." Impatience can be the result of a natural tendency to rush, an unrealistic sense of how long something will take to complete, or a lack of appreciation for the process and journey. The intent of this chapter is to explore steps that can be used to help students develop patience as a skill, to become more aware of its tremendous benefits to both music and life, and to relish the process.

SKILL CONTEXT

Most things of value and importance take time and effort to nurture. Yet now, more than ever, our students have been conditioned otherwise—a beguiling array of digital devices puts them instantly in touch with an entire world of information, people, and services. There's no waiting for anything. Those devices are at their disposal twenty-four/seven and all compete to make patience obsolete. How do we counter the patience-destroying effects of these technological distractions? We can't eradicate the opposite of patience—desire for immediacy of attainment—but the study of music can come to the rescue by helping to teach our students the value and virtue of patience. Music is a highly effective vehicle for such a process. *Patience, like most other skills, must be practiced in order to improve.* The awareness of that bit of information is something few of my students demonstrate when they begin studying with me in their freshman year. In music, learning to play an instrument well ultimately requires understanding the role and workings of patience at a deep level and being able to put it into practice daily.

After a few lessons, teachers get a pretty good idea of their students' patience levels. If a student shows a particular deficiency in that area, the teacher may wish to include some time on that topic during their weekly lessons, starting with a simple explanation of patience and its benefits to music and life.

Exercises in applying patience should first, naturally, happen through the study of an applied instrument. This will help students experience how beneficial this skill can be to their music-making and, later, allow them to see a clear connection to its importance to other disciplines.

SKILL DEFINITION

Although patience scarcely needs to be defined, here's my easy-to-remember definition for the context of the music lesson: Patience is being able to slow down to the point where details are not overlooked, but recognized and absorbed, all the while enjoying the process and not fixating on the end result. In a more philosophical sense, patience has been described as "the power of now."[4] That phrase is actually a book title by Eckhart Tolle and means, in part, to accept and embrace the present moment with equanimity and to become more aware of all that the present moment contains. To do so requires being both calm and receptive.

SKILL BREAKDOWN

To make patience a little easier for the student to grasp as a concept, I have broken this skill into a few components. Students are practicing patience when they:

1. Can consciously and effectively slow down, overcoming their tendency to rush and ignore details.
2. Are able to take in and manage details while consciously slowing down.
3. Become more comfortable with and enjoy the task at hand.
4. Value accuracy and progress over speeding to the final destination.

II. TONIC KEY
Learn to Apply the Skill to Music

I. ASSESSING YOUR STUDENTS' LEVELS OF IMPATIENCE

Ask your student to intently practice a problem spot during their lesson for at least three or four minutes. Take careful note of their actions because much will be revealed. Does the student cut corners on details, do they move on before any progress is made, do they play faster than control allows, are they unable to demonstrate good problem-solving, or do they pretend to themselves that something is done when it isn't? Once you have evaluated their patience levels, go to step two.

2. SURVEY STUDENTS' FEELINGS

Ask the student what they were feeling and thinking during the time they practiced in front of you. Did they feel impatient, were they thinking negatively, did their mind wander, did they lose interest, did they find it hard to focus on the details? If they answered yes to some of those questions or if any of those examples were visible during step one, the student may require some patience-building work and should continue to the following steps.

3. CONTINUALLY SELF-MONITOR

Monitoring is critical to the practice of patience. It involves a cycle of consistent mental reminders to slow down to the point where details are fully noted and accuracy is exercised—this step is crucial. Remind your students to continually focus on these primary objectives while practicing patience: staying in the present, valuing detail, savoring the practice process, and refraining from making negative self-judgments. (I will say more on these objectives later.)

Students must remain consistently vigilant to the monitoring cycle—because, as we know, old habits are stubborn and can easily return. Frequent reminders from the teacher may be necessary to keep a student on track in this process and to ingrain the new habit. To help students gain greater perspective on the process of patience and their own tendencies, explain to them that it is natural and entirely human to feel impatience—it's just something that can be managed. Practicing patience really is about *managing* a specific feeling or tendency, not eradicating it entirely.

4. STOP NEGATIVE SELF-JUDGEMENTS

If a student's self-talk includes, "Oh, I will never be good enough to play this well" or, "I can't be very talented because this piece just isn't improving"—they are unknowingly feeding their impatience, among other things. Those negative self-statements play into the impatience quotient because they strongly imply, why bother? And further, that student might have convinced themselves through that negative self-talk that it doesn't matter how they practice because things probably won't improve much anyway. So, it is best to simply ask your student to refrain from making negative self-judgments—reminding them of how unproductive that habit is. Suggest that instead of making negative self-comments, especially when a passage doesn't seem to improve quickly enough, the student might say (in self-talk) something like, "Wow, this is taking longer than I thought it would, but that's OK because it's going to be learned very securely when

I finally get it." They might also reinforce their statement with, "I really enjoy the process of practicing my instrument—I feel fortunate to be doing something I love on a daily basis."

To help students with patience issues that result in self-imposed negativity, ask them to promise to use only positive, self-reinforcing self-statements during their practice—especially when they *least* feel like it. In time, a new habit will be established and the student will feel greater comfort and ease with practicing patience.

The use of the basic meditation exercise of focusing on the breath (found in Chapter Two, Focus) can go a long way in helping students to develop patience. By engaging in this practice, they are consciously overlooking the mental chatter that helps to "fuel" impatience.

5. ENJOY THE PROCESS

Learning to practice with patience is not an overnight process. Help your students understand how important it is to them that they try to accept and become more comfortable with their own natural pace. Remind them that it is not just about how long it takes to master a tough section or memorize a piece; it is the ability to engage in and appreciate the "what" and the "how" of the process itself. (This includes the careful taking apart of a section of music, the slow and methodical practice, the awareness and importance of incremental progress, etc.) Suggest to your student that finding a way to enjoy even one aspect of a tough practice session will go a long way to improving patience levels. In some instances, that advice can pose quite a challenge for a student, especially if a passage requires a good deal of repetition and tenacity over time. However, that one aspect could be: I really enjoy playing the piano, or, I love the sounds it makes, or, I like the feel of my hands moving over the keys, or, I like seeing the progress I make when I really apply myself (no matter how incremental).

Change is often the result of the transformative power of patience well-applied. Patience, therefore, is an extremely important component in the music-learning process because, as we all know, some pieces take months or years to master and reach maturity. Once the skill of patience is well in hand, a student's journey of taking a piece from first look to performance can be both very productive and enjoyable indeed.

III. PIVOT CHORD
Prepare to Transpose the Skill to a Non-Music Application

Once students have a clear idea of the benefits of patience and have demonstrated some success using it during their music practice, they are ready to apply it in other areas of life. Don't assume that your students will naturally make this beneficial connection by themselves. Now you can prepare your students to apply (take) the music steps for patience to a non-music area. By adding this transference step, you significantly widen the traditional parameters of the music lesson and provide your students with a tool that benefits not only their musical performance, but *any* aspect of their lives. This step creates a major shift in the thinking of how the traditional music lesson should transpire and introduces a whole new range of possibilities for teachers to explore for the benefit of their students. As I mention often, it is both my conviction and experience that exercising a universal skill in multiple areas/disciplines dramatically increases one's ability in understanding and applying it overall. Indeed, the practice of transference heightens one's awareness of the possible interconnections throughout life.

To begin, ask your students if there are any areas in their lives where impatience plays a negative role. Have any of their friends ever felt the brunt of their impatience? Are they aware of any instance where their impatience has negatively affected them in some way? A student might reply that they feel the negative effects of impatience in many aspects of their daily lives, including: standing in line at a store, waiting in traffic, or bailing out of a potentially big opportunity because they just couldn't "stick with it."

Once you have started your students thinking about patience as a universal skill and a necessary tool that can be used in any situation, they are ready to actively transfer the skill.

IV. TRANSPOSITION
Actively Transpose the Skill to a Non-Music Application

Through the process of transference, use the same steps found above in the music application to demonstrate how patience can be practiced in non-music areas. Remember, you are the "patience transfer coach" (not the therapist!). Rein in the length of responses that may result in this section by remaining focused on the same questions you used to assess students' patience in music.

1. ASSESS LEVELS OF IMPATIENCE

During your discussion, a student might relay that their impatience sometimes gets them "too wound up and it is not a good feeling." The teacher might then ask, "What was the situation and what was the result of that impatience?" The student responds that it usually happens during their part-time job as a bagger at a grocery store, saying "The shift never ends soon enough and I am constantly thinking about what else I would rather be doing." At this point the problem area has been identified and the next step can be applied.

2. BRIEFLY SURVEY FEELINGS

Ask the student to take note of the feelings that arise as a result of his work at the grocery store; they may include agitation, tenseness, negativity, unrest, anger, etc. Then have the student apply simple logic by asking: what did any of those feelings do to improve the situation? "Nothing," the student will invariably reply. From a purely logical view, feeling impatient does nothing to speed up the bagging process; it just makes it *less* bearable. However, logic alone will often not be

enough to keep impatience from continuing to be an issue for some. It requires another step.

3. CONSTANTLY MONITOR

Once a student can pinpoint the emotions that arise when feeling impatient, no matter the situation, it should now be their goal to make a conscious choice to let those unconstructive emotions go or not dwell on them. Identifying a concrete emotion or feeling is integral to countering the negative effects of impatience. So, when a student senses they are feeling the symptoms of impatience (becoming tense or angry or nothing is progressing fast enough) while at their job, they can specifically counter those feelings by first acknowledging them and then working to dwell on them less and less. They can start by recalling a peaceful scene or by focusing on deep and steady breathing. Or, they can focus on being in the moment without assigning any characterizations to their work and just being observant, or they can simply chat with customers as they come and go. This practice of diverting or redirecting one's mind is explained more fully in step five, below.

4. STOP NEGATIVE SELF-JUDGEMENTS

It is easy to be negative towards oneself, no matter the task or situation—the student might feel that they deserve to be working at a better, higher paying job and that there must be some personal failing as a reason. Negative self-talk can quickly douse any hope of achieving any semblance of patience. For the music student doing his part-time grocery bagging job, a good start would be recalling what his teacher had said during the prior music application of this step: that negative judgement has no good purpose and should be avoided if possible. Like many habits, this one can take time to modify and ultimately to change. Once the student has made some headway, they can proceed to step five, and try to find *something* to enjoy about the process.

5. MAKING THE TASK MORE ENJOYABLE

Some students may be surprised when we tell them that they actually have a good bit of control over how they mentally process a situation—they can make it a positive or negative experience. This mental course change may not be possible in every task or function, but it should be a priority. In the case of the student working part-time in the grocery store, perhaps some small talk with customers at the check-out lane might become the one redeeming aspect of the job. Or, what if the student connected their knowledge of efficient movement at the piano keyboard to efficient movement as a grocery bagger, including constantly trying to find more efficient ways to grasp and move items with less effort and physical movement? Making sure students apply this step during any task where impatience tends to lurk can go a long way in creating a path to less stress and better work results.

As with all the chapters in this book, the application examples above are not intended to be an exhaustive study on any one particular skill. Rather, each chapter presents an introduction to one individual skill, its practical use within the music lesson, and, finally, some examples of its transference to life. I can't encourage teachers enough to feel free to exercise their imaginations in working out the best way to approach the skill transfer component of the lesson with their students. Use the general direction of non-music application examples as a springboard for your own way of helping your students see skills as universal tools that have endless applications.

V. RECAP
Revisit the Skill in Music

THE CROSS-TRAINING BENEFIT

There is a great benefit to be gained from learning a universal skill and then applying it to both music and non-music use. Through varied applications of the skill, the transference practice forges a deeper understanding and enables a more nuanced approach. For example, a student studying wood-carving would find that using a mallet and chisel on stone is very different from using similar tools on wood. In each case, however, use in one situation can inform and benefit use in the other. Perhaps, tapping on a wood chisel created better control in the user's hands that later benefitted their work on stone. The same sort of benefit can be had by applying a universal skill in both music *and* in non-music situations. For example, plenty of musicians are involved in sports—this provides fertile ground for cross-training opportunities through shared concept/idea applications. Perhaps a music teacher introduced the concept of cross-training to one of their students who also swims competitively in school. That student is now on the alert to apply that concept wherever possible. One day, her swim coach introduced the technique of interval training to improve endurance and speed in the pool. After applying this new training technique in her swimming practices, she soon realized that it could also benefit her violin practice—especially because she tended to practice for hours at a time without a break. Once she began taking breaks from playing her violin, every 30 minutes or so, she immediately became aware that her practice efficiency improved: her mind was more rested and retained more information and her arms and hands also felt fresher and more responsive. This illustrates the great potential of the cross-training idea—where using a concept, idea, or universal skill in one area can benefit another area.

VI. QUESTIONS FOR REFLECTION

1. Have your students seen an increase in their level of patience in their practice and life in general?
2. Are they now able to better monitor and regulate their levels of impatience as the need arises?
3. Have your students seen an increase in their ability to get things done more efficiently, effectively, and comfortably as a result of their increased patience levels?
4. Do your students seem to have a better overall sense of well-being by consciously monitoring their patience levels?
5. Where does each of your students feel their increased level of patience has benefitted them the most: in their practice or life?

VII. SUGGESTED READING

Easwaran, Eknath. *Patience: The Little Book of Inner Strength*. Canada: Nilgiri Press, 2010.

O'Donnell, James. *How to Become Patient*. CreateSpace Independent Publishing Platform, 2016.

Ryan, M. J. *The Power of Patience: How this Old-Fashioned Virtue Can Improve Your Life*. San Francisco, CA: Conari Press, 2013.

Souchester, Greg. *How to Be More Patient: An Essential Guide to Replacing Impatience with Patience*. Miafn, LLC, 2015.

VIII. REFERENCES

1. M. J. Ryan, *The Power of Patience: How This Old-Fashioned Virtue Can Improve Your Life* (San Francisco, CA: Conari Press, 2013), 5.
2. Allan Lokos, *Patience, The Art of Living Peacefully* (New York, NY: Jeremy P. Tarcher/Penguin, 2012), 18.
3. Albert Einstein, *Bite-Size Einstein: Quotations on Just About Everything from the Greatest Mind of the Twentieth Century,* compiled by Jerry Mayer and John P. Holmes (New York, NY: MacMillan, 1996), 17.
4. Eckhard Tolle, *The Power of Now: A Guide to Spiritual Enlightenment* (Novato, CA: The New World Library, 1999), 35.

IX. NOTES

CHAPTER 4

CRITICAL THINKING

"Critical thinking is the disciplined art of ensuring that you use the best thinking you are capable of in any set of circumstances."
—Richard Paul and Linda Elder.[1]

"We do not always need to be an expert in a subject to evaluate an argument."
—Stella Cottrell.[2]

"It ain't what you don't know that gets you into trouble. It's what you know for sure that just ain't so."
—Mark Twain.[3]

I. SKILL IMPORTANCE, CONTEXT, DEFINITION, AND BREAKDOWN

SKILL IMPORTANCE AND CONTEXT

This skill is best introduced to the more advanced music student—one who has become more sophisticated in the interpretational elements of the music-making process.

One of the hallmarks of a top-flight musician is that their every musical utterance seems very clear, well-defined, and original. Sometimes, even their sound or way of playing immediately distinguishes who they are—the great pianist Horowitz had that quality, so did the violinist Heifetz. Most musicians would agree that achieving such clarity of idea and individuality through one's playing is the holy grail of the profession. But how does a musician develop that level of musical clarity and individuality? Do those qualities come from conscious decision, is it purely instinctual, or a little of both? And, if it is conscious, what might the thought process be?

I believe that the critical thinking process can help musicians significantly build those elusive and coveted qualities. I think that the ability to project clear intent and a highly individualized way of playing *is* something we can consciously develop and is not something left to chance. At the very least, applying critical thinking to practice and performance can help students become more confident and expressive musicians.

The musician who examines and questions every aspect of their playing and *why* they think the way they do about music gets to know themselves and their musical processes very well. I believe that this familiarity provides increased interpretive options to the musician: it enables them to clearly view the full inventory of their expressive and technical arsenal, and thus it opens up more possibilities in how it could be used, developed, or modified. Once a musician has arrived at the point where they know *how* and, most importantly, *why* they have arrived at each musical decision in a piece—where every note they play is a true reflection of their musical thinking, where honesty to the score is evident, and where nothing is happenstance—they are truly expressing themselves at a level which is both authentic and well-informed.

In addition to using critical thinking during musical preparation and practice, there are opportunities for practical applications of the skill throughout every aspect of life—this will be covered in the second half of this chapter in the transposition section. For thorough application of this skill in music, musicians must analyze, conceptualize, question, synthesize, and evaluate every facet of their practice and performance, including all interpretive and technical aspects. This in-depth approach to music-making also includes questioning, reflection, observation, reason, communication, and experience. Ultimately, the critical thinking process used to guide and form an individualistic and artistic interpretation must be applied within the context of the composer's intentions, so as not to stray too far afield and distort.

In my experience, I have found critical thinking lacking in my incoming students. I continually ask each of my freshman students "How did you arrive at that interpretation or why did you play it that way?" I ask because I want to get a sense of how they arrived at a decision, because I believe every musical utterance should come from an informed thought process and not be happenstance. Most of my freshman students have been unable to offer any reasons or rationale other than they "just felt it that way" or "hadn't given much thought to it." (I am well aware that "just feeling it that way" has its merits—especially if one has good instincts—but I believe conscious decisions should be very much a part of the interpretive process, too.) My students' responses have been a clear indication to me that they were not giving much thought to the choices they made when learning and interpreting their scores. To remediate, I immediately start helping them change this unproductive habit: I ask them to think about adopting an approach where every sound they produce comes from a decision and where every musical input is purposeful. *That*, I tell them, is the beginning of meaningful and individualized performance—because then it is truly a reflection of their thinking. This can only spring from a process of thinking deeply and critically about music.

Later, through coaching and practice, my students are able to reply quite differently to the same question of why they made the choices they have in performing a piece; perhaps responding "I lengthened that rest to create a greater sense of surprise with the double forte chord that immediately follows." Or, "I intentionally went against traditional performance practice when playing this Bach piece to make the point that if the composer had a modern grand piano, he surely would have utilized its full expressive capabilities." When I hear comments like that, whether or not I agree, I know my students are thinking more about the process of making music by making choices through a disciplined mental approach of conceptualizing, synthesizing, analyzing, evaluating, etc.

Before we get to the application, let's first get on the same page when it comes to a definition of critical thinking.

SKILL DEFINITION AND BREAKDOWN

Although most of us have a pretty good idea of what critical thinking means, I am including two definitions for clarity and perspective. In one, critical thinking is defined by writers Paul and Elder as "The intellectually disciplined process of actively and skillfully conceptualizing, applying, analyzing, synthesizing, and/or evaluating information gathered from, or generated by, observation, experience, reflection, reasoning, or communication, as a guide to belief and action."[4]

Another definition (this one in four parts), from Brookfield's *Teaching for Critical Thinking* book, helps to expand the notion of critical thinking: "(1) identifying the assumptions that frame our thinking and determine our actions, (2) checking out the degree to which these assumptions are accurate and valid, (3) looking at our ideas and decisions (intellectual, organizational, and personal) from several different perspectives, and (4) on the basis of this, taking informed actions."[5]

Critical thinking also involves reflecting on the process of *how* one thinks—known as meta-cognition. For example, this might involve a musician recalling and questioning the rationale behind their musical decisions, including: Why did I play it that way? Was I influenced by hearing another interpretation? How close or far am I to the traditional performance practice of this composer? Am I totally relying on the suggestions of my teacher? The process might also entail questions such as: How informed do I wish to be before making a choice? What steps might I take in such a process? What will be my sources? Those questions help a student begin determining how to gain a more genuine approach to interpreting music and to creating their own individual voice. This can only happen if students' *own* thought processes and choices are driving the equation.

Critical thinking is self-guided thinking. Steps—a set protocol if you will—are necessary to gain fluency in this thinking process to avoid distorted, biased, or uninformed thought that may otherwise result—potentially degrading the end result or product. To help my students think more critically about music and how they will go about practicing and crafting an interpretation, I use the four principles found in the second set of definitions above.

To apply these principles, let's use a well-known music example and see where they can be applied. The opening line of the Beethoven *Pathétique* piano sonata, Op.13, first movement, is a good one because it asks the pianist to manage a great many dynamic, rhythmic, and articulation elements in quick succession.

II. TONIC KEY
Learn to Apply the Skill to Music

1. FIRST IDENTIFY THE ASSUMPTIONS THAT FRAME OUR THINKING AND DETERMINE OUR ACTIONS

Example: Assumptions can pervade every aspect of musical thought and yet their genesis may often be a mystery. How often have we asked our students: "Why did you play it that way?" only to receive the common (and disappointing) reply, "I don't know." Often, assumptions simply result from a lack of examination—something happens in a certain way while playing and it becomes accepted. For instance, I have heard countless piano students slur the last note in the bass clef (a 32nd-note) of the first measure of the *Pathétique* to the first note of the second measure. Yet, it is clearly not indicated that way; there is no slur marked. The common reason that students incorrectly slur this: it just falls into the hand that way and they have not elevated their ears and/or score reading abilities enough to catch it. That is an example of how happenstance or an assumption (having heard it that way before) in music can inadvertently shape an interpretation. We also know that students often just "let their hands play" with little-to-no thought involved. Other times, their playing just follows their own assumptions, such as "I like it that way"— something I have often heard my students say.

Critical thinking applies to all components in the music-making process, including the choice of what performance edition to use; students must be taught things like performance practice and how to view different editions, or how would they know otherwise? It is very important for teachers to ask their students questions: Why did you play that way? How do you know that way of playing is stylistically correct? How do you formulate an identity in your interpretations? And then help them on the path to answers. By doing this, teachers begin demonstrating to their students the importance of giving conscious, questioning thought to every aspect of music-making and how this way of thinking leads them to informed decisions. It also leads students more sure-footedly to authentic, personal performances by helping them get into the habit of thinking about *how* they arrive at the decisions they make in music. Critical thinking steps, then, give the student a mechanism to combat their former habit of making uninformed decisions and an awareness of the insidious way assumptions can pervade, take hold, and ultimately, form an interpretation of a piece without any basis.

As you begin this chapter with your student, you will be helping to prepare them for the time and effort it will take to think through every measure of music they will be practicing and performing. But assure them that their efforts will be rewarded in the increased assuredness and musical competency that they will gain.

2. CHECKING OUT THE DEGREE TO WHICH ASSUMPTIONS ARE ACCURATE AND VALID

Example: Now that you have alerted your students to the possibility that many of their assumptions in music may be incorrect or unfounded and require revising, they must begin a habitual process of carefully checking their assumptions. A good start involves evaluating and questioning the validity of their sources (if any): Where is their information coming from? Is it from a reputable or questionable resource? For example: Have they assumed that their heavily edited edition of the Beethoven sonatas reinforces the composer's intentions?

Would checking it against an Urtext edition be the very first step in making a secure determination? Yes, it would.

Example: Perhaps the student heard a performance of a piece from an artist online that they admire and wish to emulate. Before accepting the performance as a model for their own development, however, wouldn't it be a good exercise to question aspects of the online artist's performance first? For example, how does the online performance practice coincide with what the student has learned through an Urtext edition? Do the tempos seem ridiculously fast? Are the rubatos over-done or too prevalent? How does the pedaling compare to what is indicated? Are inner voices ignored, brought out, or over-emphasized? After listening to the performance a few times and contemplating these questions and others, the student could still choose to emulate that online artist's performance. However, they will be doing so from an informed point of view where conscious decisions were made. Perhaps the student ultimately chooses to consciously break with some norms and stretch the parameters of traditional performance practice. Critical thinking will provide the student with parameters which, when known, can then be deliberately stretched or broken—but now with perspective. The important thing here is that the student made a conscious decision, not an uninformed one. This could be their start of intentionally crafting a more conscious and individual approach to playing.

3. LOOKING AT OUR IDEAS AND DECISIONS FROM DIFFERENT
   PERSPECTIVES (INTELLECTUAL, ORGANIZATIONAL, AND PERSONAL)

Example: Here, the student considers an interpretive decision through different filters—whether or not to dramatically augment the loud and soft dynamics in the opening page of the *Pathétique* sonata and why. How accurately will they employ every rhythm? How much, if any, rubato will be used, and where? These processes also employ problem-solving, trial and error, and experimentation. Ultimately, the final selection is made through reflecting on multiple interpretive variants and how decisions will be made.

Here are some illustrations of how the student might use these three different perspectives for filtering their ideas and decisions:

- an intellectual perspective allows the student to draw from and reflect upon scholarly sources to help guide them toward interpretive decisions. The student might conclude, for example, that their choice to augment the dynamic contrasts in the opening of the *Pathétique* sonata has merit after having read that Beethoven was always looking for more power and range in his pianos.

- an organizational perspective may include prioritizing the merits of a particular decision. Perhaps a student rationalizes that even though the pianos of Beethoven's time could not match the dynamic range of the modern concert grand today, the fact that the composer most likely would have utilized those louder dynamics had he possessed such an instrument might ultimately nudge the student to augment the dynamic range beyond what the composer indicated in the score.

- a personal perspective might include a student prioritizing their own natural interpretational tendencies or preferences (over scholarly sources and accepted performance practice). This may include "amping up" the dynamic contrasts in the *Pathétique's* opening page and/or expanding their use of rubato beyond the norms of performance practice. Ultimately, an honest, accurate, and yet still individual interpretation comes from a marriage of melding facts (derived through critical thinking) and intuition.

Applying multiple perspectives, such as the three listed immediately above, can help students improve their chances of developing more informed, creative, and individual interpretations of a score.

4. TAKING INFORMED ACTIONS BASED UPON SUBSTANTIAL EVIDENCE

Example: Ultimately, a student must make decisions based upon their findings. How are they going to approach playing the *Pathétique* piano sonata? Usually, they work through a synthesis of learning information from their teacher, reading about performance practice, hearing performances of others, and trusting their own convictions. The results of that synthesis might include using sparse pedal and very dry, defined articulations throughout to portray some of the hallmarks of the classical style. They might also include amplifying the elements of lyricism. Those choices, then, are not randomly made, but based on multiple sources and thought.

By thinking critically about the scores they are studying (Urtext or edited), students begin making their own informed choices regarding their interpretations, not solely relying on those of their teachers or performers they have heard. This is how students begin to advance their individual thought processes regarding music making, and it can lead to developing an individual, distinctive voice. Making informed decisions also helps students build high levels of confidence, because they will know how and why they arrived at the choices they made. Just as an architect must give specific thought to every square foot in a building proposal, including design, materials, lighting, construction, efficiency, and specific usage, why shouldn't a musician give the same kind of thought to the contents of every measure? They are, like the architect, drawing up a blueprint to render an eventual product—in this case, a performance.

III. PIVOT CHORD
Prepare to Transpose the Skill to a Non-Music Application

Here, we prepare to apply (take) the steps for critical thinking in music to critical thinking in non-music areas. As mentioned often in this book, just because a student has learned to apply a universal skill in music performance doesn't mean they will automatically transfer that skill to a non-music application (consequently losing the potential additional benefits!). To ensure this skill transference succeeds, students usually need their teacher's help alerting them to the importance of this process—encouraging them to use a particular skill in multiple areas of life because of how beneficial it can be to them. It is also important to reiterate that the music teacher does *not* need to be an expert in the non-music applications of critical thinking. The example below will serve as a basic template and demonstrate that the teacher guides the student through the non-music skill application using the same basic steps and questions they used in the music application above.

IV. TRANSPOSITION
Actively Transpose the Skill to a Non-Music Application

NON-MUSIC APPLICATION OF CRITICAL THINKING

To start the transference process, ask your student, Oscar, where he might use his newly-learned critical thinking skill outside music? Has he been in a situation where he needs to make an important decision and was tempted to just go with his intuition, or maybe with information he heard secondhand? Did he have a nagging feeling that caused him to want more information before making that important decision? Perhaps Oscar just turned eighteen and was planning to vote in a coming election. Will he vote according to his friends' or family's convictions, or come to his own conclusions based upon information from additional sources? This would be a perfect opportunity for him to apply the critical thinking skills he first applied to his music study and performance. (Of course, there need be no actual discussion of politics with your student to help them transfer their critical thinking skills into research for this application—just the critical thinking process itself.) Here are some non-music application examples that the teacher can use as a template to get started:

I. WE MUST FIRST IDENTIFY THE ASSUMPTIONS THAT FRAME OUR THINKING AND DETERMINE OUR ACTIONS

Using the voting example, Oscar must consider what opinions and assumptions he already has, if any, regarding his current choice of a candidate or candidates and how those opinions were formed. How did he come to his conclusions? What sources did he use? Was it just one source such as a local paper or radio talk show host, or was it a few sources, including some credible, nationally known ones?

2. CHECKING OUT THE DEGREE TO WHICH ASSUMPTIONS ARE ACCURATE AND VALID

Oscar must now make the effort to check his assumptions for accuracy and also consider learning more detail and breadth of information regarding the candidates in a particular race. This step usually requires the most effort and, consequently, is often overlooked, purposely avoided, or done superficially. In the case of picking a candidate for some elected office, Oscar will have to do a little research on the candidate's particular platform and then compare it to his initial assumptions. What source will he use? Will it be more than one? Do his sources square with one another, or do they contain discrepancies? If so, what then? Perhaps a third source might be needed in order to confirm the validity of one of the other two sources. Perhaps, after doing some research, Oscar found that the candidate he was initially hoping to vote for did not support the issues most important to him. Oscar's realization that doing research provided a clearer view of a candidate gave him a greater appetite for using critical thinking in important decision-making in the future.

3. LOOKING AT OUR IDEAS AND DECISIONS FROM DIFFERENT PERSPECTIVES (INTELLECTUAL, ORGANIZATIONAL, AND PERSONAL)

This is perhaps the most sophisticated of the four steps and requires significant maturity of thought. In this step, Oscar must take time to thoroughly examine his decisions on choosing a political candidate from varying perspectives. For example, how biased is he when it comes to the arts? Perhaps, as a student musician, he finds himself over-valuing that area when it came to researching his candidate. Perhaps his candidate has a strong record on the arts but a poor one on other important issues. Knowing that, would that candidate now be a good choice? Many platforms, Oscar concludes, are just as important as the arts to the general good of the community. Here, he realized that he was using only a personal perspective to make a decision on choosing his political candidate and did not consider the bigger overall picture and greater benefit to society. Regardless of the end choice in this instance, Oscar made the effort to become more informed and aware, especially with regard to his own biases.

4. TAKING INFORMED ACTIONS BASED UPON SUBSTANTIAL EVIDENCE

Now that Oscar has carefully examined all his information and checked it for validity and accuracy (using multiple, reputable sources), making a choice on a candidate and acting upon it at the ballot box is his final step. There are no more lingering questions as to whether or not the choice for his candidate was the right one or not. Through critical thinking, making informed decisions now becomes more comfortable and reliable and will serve Oscar immeasurably throughout life. And yes, making informed choices requires more effort than uninformed choices.

Here again, the music teacher has taken a skill that was initially used to improve music-making and transferred it outside the boundaries of the traditional music lesson for the greater benefit of their students. Once students have applied the critical thinking skill outside the field of music, they understand the skill on a deeper level, largely due to the insights that diverse applications reveal.

This practice of teaching a diverse use of universal skills through music instruction gives the lesson a whole new dimension and potential because it can now benefit all areas of a student's life.

V. RECAP
Revisit the Skill in Music

KEEP IN MIND HOW MANY UNIVERSAL SKILLS ARE USED IN MUSIC

The music teacher is in a unique position to teach a wide variety of universal skills because the study of music provides such fertile ground through which to learn them—largely because so many of those very skills are required to play well. Of those many skills, critical thinking (closely allied with problem-solving) is certainly at the very top in importance. Most students will soon recognize this skill as a highly functional and important tool for all of life. Now that Oscar has exercised his critical thinking skills in a non-music application, his teacher encourages him to reflect on how that process can "circle back" and further benefit his music study and performance. Could the experience of carefully researching political candidates for an election have provided him with a deeper understanding and renewed conviction of applying the same process, but this time more emphatically, to his music-making endeavors? Could gaining a significant breadth of knowledge of performance practice and other historical information lead him to a more authentic interpretation of a particular composer? Could it also lead him to better-develop a creative and engaging recital that might involve period costumes, theater, and narration? Absolutely!

As with any of these chapters, the music teacher is encouraged to pick and choose which universal skill for transference might be most effective for a student at a given time, to whatever extent they and the student feel comfortable. At the very least, the skill transference concept can be introduced to your students without going into much detail; that alone can sometimes be enough to start a student thinking about experimenting with the idea. I encourage the creative use of the concepts presented here; my examples are meant to be starting points, a springboard upon which to extend and further develop your own. By all means, expand on these ideas and create your own paths!

VI. QUESTIONS FOR REFLECTION

1. Can you see a new or clearer path toward helping students develop the more elusive elements in music instruction: expression and individual voice?
2. How much has the critical thinking process helped your students in studying and performing music?
3. Has it made learning music more accurate and thorough for them?
4. Has it helped create a pathway toward a more expressive, individualized interpretation?
5. Has it helped your students become more confident and secure in their performances?
6. Does critical thinking help them unveil more depth and detail while learning?
7. Ask your students what it does to their confidence to arrive at an important decision using the critical thinking process (compared with their previous process or lack of one). Do the end results justify the time and energy in making a well-researched decision?
8. Did your students experience any further music benefits after applying this skill in non-music applications?

VII. SUGGESTED READING

Bassham, Gregory, William Irwin, Henry Nardone, James M. Wallace. *Critical Thinking: A Student's Introduction.* New York, NY: McGraw-Hill, 2013.

Jackson, Debra and Paul Newberry. *Critical Thinking: A User's Manual.* United States: Wadsworth Cengage Learning, 2010.

Moore, Brooke Noel and Richard Parker. *Critical Thinking*, 12th ed. New York, NY: McGraw-Hill, 2017.

Richard, Paul and Linda Elder. *Critical Thinking: Tools for Taking Charge of Your Professional and Personal Life.* Upper Saddle River, NJ: Pearson Education, Inc., 2014.

VIII. REFERENCES

1. Paul Richard and Linda Elder, *Critical Thinking: Tools for Taking Charge of Your Professional and Personal Life* (Upper Saddle River, NJ: Pearson Education, Inc., 2014), 9.

2. Stella Cottrell, *Critical Thinking Skills: Developing Effective Analysis and Argument*, 2nd edition (New York, NY: Palgrave Macmillan, 2011), 125.

3. Dick Miller, "Family Finance: Statistics Can Be Twisted to Fool Unwary," *Boston Traveler*, June 26, 1964, 24.

4. Michael Scriven and Richard W. Paul, "Critical Thinking as Defined by the National Council for Excellence in Critical Thinking," The Foundation for Critical Thinking, https://www.criticalthinking.org/pages/defining-critical-thinking/766, 1987.

5. Stephen D. Brookfield, *Teaching for Critical Thinking: Tools and Techniques to Help Students Question Their Assumptions.* (San Francisco, CA: Jossey-Bass, 2012), 1.

IX. NOTES

CHAPTER 5

COMMUNICATION

"To add value to others, one must first value others."
—John C. Maxwell.[1]

"Getting started is usually the hardest part."
—Chuck Garcia.[2]

"When you connect with others, you position yourself to make the most of your skills and talents."
—John C. Maxwell.[3]

I. SKILL IMPORTANCE, CONTEXT, DEFINITION, AND BREAKDOWN

SKILL IMPORTANCE

We have all long heard about the importance of communicating well. Educators, from primary grades through university levels, continually promote the development of good communication skills. The ability to say or write something that clearly makes a point or conveys a needed directive can be surprisingly challenging. If we think about it, how often do we hear adults in our day-to-day lives struggle to be clear and succinct when speaking? I am frequently reminded of the difficulty and the need for communicating well when listening to my students discussing the particulars of a performance—either theirs or someone else's—in their piano performance classes. Their struggles usually revolve around not being able to be descriptive enough to define an issue—saying something like: "the middle section didn't sound quite right or very good" instead of "the middle section lacked clarity because passages were not played with enough articulation and evenness."

Clarity of communication is equally important (and challenging!) while performing music. Many freshman students come to me with poor communication skills at the piano: changes of mood are scarcely revealed; dynamic changes and levels are rarely made clear; rhythms are often less than accurate; surprising changes of key are not illuminated by any musical indication such as a slight ritard, use of rubato, or dynamic shading, etc. Specifically, their music-making lacks a compelling message. It's an issue, of course, that I seek to begin improving right away!

SKILL CONTEXT

The ability to be expressive as a musician has everything to do with the ability to communicate an idea or series of ideas. In other words, if the storyline of a piece of music does not first reside clearly in one's head, nothing much of clarity will find its way through the hands and fingers.

This chapter will speak to the close connection between communicating well in word and communicating well in music—and how each can benefit the other. Both methods of communication share many of the same principles, which will be pointed out. First, however, a few descriptive words about the art of communication itself:

SKILL DEFINITION

When I talk to my students about the necessity of communicating their ideas through performance, I always mention what Richard Worth calls the four C's of successful writing: "Concise. Compelling. Clear. Correct."[4] I like how concise and simple that definition is. Of course, these same four words can also apply to many forms of communication, including dance, art, music, speaking, or writing. Because his description is so succinct, I will use those four words to build my argument for their use in communicating well in music.

SKILL BREAKDOWN

To be **Concise** in writing (or speech) often means keeping things short and to the point; in music it can mean keeping musical objectives uncluttered (don't confuse the listener by changing a musical point of view before the section of music warrants it).

Compelling writing convinces the reader to take the author's view; in music it can mean that the performer has put across an idea so convincingly that it engages and moves the listener. In both cases, how might this be done? Primarily, it is accomplished when the presenter *really* has thought about how they were going to construct and convey their ideas and strongly believes in their message. That conviction, then, comes across as genuine emotion; something that is hard to disguise and is also quite contagious.

To be **Clear** in writing means that the message is unambiguous; this is also true in music. A sudden double forte must be powerful enough to be unmistakable, a staccato passage should not be mistaken for one merely played somewhat detached, and rubato must rendered in such a way as to be an unmistakable (though momentary) change of tempo.

Being **Correct,** depending on the discipline, can have multiple interpretations, such as a high degree of accuracy or even flawless execution when following directives. In music performance, this means that the performer essentially remains true to the composer's dictates, accurately playing the notes and rhythms while expressing a personal interpretation.

As I continually remind my students, the importance of communicating well can't be stressed enough—in music or any art form. In my estimation, as musicians, it is our very reason for being! Most of us spend a great deal of our time each day in some form of communication: speaking to a friend, writing an email, or, in the case of a musician, performing music. In all instances there is a sender and a receiver. For musicians, the receiver of their message is often a group of people. So, why not make an art of communication and practice it daily?

As music teachers, we continually work to help our students understand the importance of communicating the essence of the score to an audience—delivering emotional content based upon the composer's myriad markings. Toward that goal, we spend a tremendous amount of time helping our students master expressive musical elements in their playing, including phrasing, dynamics, articulations, etc. But it doesn't end there; it is only the beginning because there has to be something *behind* those elements for real communication to take place. There has to be some overarching point of view, an opinion, for the musical goal to become manifest and affect the listener. Primarily, there has to be a *what* and a *how* determination for something to be effectively communicated. For example, a conductor might have these questions when working up a score: Is their primary goal to enrapture the audience with the beauty of the A section and astonish and surprise them by the massive dynamic changes of the B section? In another score, could it be the relentless drive of the motor rhythms and unwavering tempo that they primarily wish for the audience to experience? In each case, how could the conductor accomplish those musical ideas without first having a clear sense of exactly *what* she wanted to say and *how* she would say it? Although communication is primarily thought of as something to be directed toward others, it first must be to oneself. Once the *what* is inwardly clear, *how* will the conductor express their goals to their ensemble so that they are clear, concise, correct, and compelling?

I like to think about communicating through music in the same way as communicating through writing or speech. I find it helps me to think more clearly about what it is I want to inspire my audience to think and feel. Surprisingly, that very important dimension of performing had never really occurred to me before my twenties. Until then, I pretty much thought along these lines, if at all: "I'll play very expressively, feeling it as I go and hope my audience likes it." OK, but far too vague for anything of real value to be expressed. Communicating in a more specific way—including what I wanted to say and how—just wasn't on my radar back then. However, once I started thinking about communication, I also had to begin thinking about *who* the audience might be, *what* feelings I would choose to express to them, and *how* I would accomplish this.

This led me to thinking about my performance as a *product*, and how it might be better-defined. (I hadn't thought that way before, either.) I soon discovered that the "who," "what," and "how" were all a pretty important part of a performance and, with that realization, connected deeply to the idea of communication! Imagine an owner of a business spending millions of dollars on developing a new product without researching or thinking much about their target audience—it would be unheard of. But how different is that from doing nothing more than selecting a group of pieces (just because you like them) and then practicing for months and months to perform them for some undefined audience, with little thought to your specific communication goals? With no more thought than that, what possible outcome could take place, other than pure happenstance? To be effective communicators, we must do more. In the next section, you will read about some communication skills you can use to help your students express themselves more fully at their instruments and, later in the transference section, in life as well.

One last point: when students are encouraged to start thinking of their performances as a "product," it may focus them more on the question of *what* audiences want to hear or *how* the concert will be presented. Do audiences want to hear yet another recital in the usual standard format or perhaps something with a new twist? Thinking more about what an audience might want to hear or connect with is something musicians may want to be thinking more about these days. It's no secret—audiences want something new in their concerts, and successful communication will play a big role.

II. TONIC KEY
Learn to Apply the Skill to Music

THE BASIC ELEMENTS FOR COMMUNICATING WELL ARE UNIVERSAL

Well-communicated music involves many of the same specific expressive and communicative processes found in excellent spoken communication, including dynamics (for indicating importance and maintaining interest), tempo and rubato (for pacing and making points), and articulation (clarity of expression and understanding). By augmenting a student's sense of what good communication skills are—including helping them see the shared intersections between word and music—they'll gain a perspective that can benefit both their music and non-music modes of communication.

COMPONENTS OF COMMUNICATION

1. WHO IS YOUR AUDIENCE?

Once you have an idea who the audience will be, you are in a much better position to communicate more effectively. For example: as a medical doctor, you will write for fellow MDs very differently than for the general public. In the same vein, if you are a pianist planning a recital for the general public, you would most likely program differently than when playing a program at a conservatory of music. Impress upon your students that the success of good communication skills depends a lot on knowing *who* the receiver is. How would a recital consisting of the last three Schubert Piano Sonatas go over (no matter how great the pianist was) for the general public? In this case, it might be difficult to sustain the public's interest. Instead, wouldn't more diversity in programming do a great deal for keeping that general audience more engaged?

Exercise: Ask your students to try to determine more clearly who their next audience will be and how that knowledge may affect programming. If they will be performing in a retirement home, they might consider the age group. At this writing, that might include programming popular melodies of the 1940s and 50s and perhaps even some well-known hymns scattered among their classical pieces. If your student is playing for a war veteran's gathering, it might be a great idea to include a medley of Army, Navy, Air Force, and Marine arrangements. For that venue, your student could also put together a series of marches from classical music composers to better fit the overall tone of the gathering. Make sure your students understand that people always appreciate hearing something they know. How does one find that out? Well, by asking. Perhaps your student might have a short meeting with the program director of the retirement community or nursing home, during which time they specifically ask about music selection and what the residents seem to like. Crafting a program that includes keeping the audience in mind will make a big difference in a student's ability to connect and communicate!

2. WHAT'S YOUR PURPOSE?

As I mentioned, for years I performed concert programs for the general public without thinking much about their purpose, other than the fact that I wanted to play a program and I chose music I liked. My repertoire choice back then was largely (habitually) shaped by my past degree-related goals—including selections from the usual three or four style periods all packaged in the traditional format (walk out somberly, bow, sit, play, repeat). What if I had asked myself some additional questions: Why am I playing this program? What is the overall goal? Who is my audience? Have I ever even thought to try and figure out what they may be listening to? How can I make my program interesting to them without compromising my performance? These questions never came up for me (or for my classmates as far as I could tell). As I now know, the answer to each helps define the process of refining intent and is crucial to the overall effectiveness of communication.

Exercise: Encourage your students to think more about their next program using the questions just mentioned above. If it is repertoire for a competition or a degree recital run-through, then programming is usually tightly controlled by the institutions' requirements. If, however, the program they are planning is more for entertainment's sake, such as a paid performance for The Lions Club, then intent and, consequently, programming will be entirely different, all based upon communication with the institution. A lecture recital would have yet another purpose with its own specific demands—again, built with a specific audience in mind. Whatever the purpose, once repertoire has been selected for a particular program, every section of each piece must be thought through in order to deliver maximum effect, which brings us to the student's next step: What do they think the essence of each section of each piece is, and what basic feeling or mood do they want to project? Urge them to always speak to their audiences. That person-to-person connection cannot be underestimated.

3. WHAT DO YOU WANT TO COMMUNICATE, AND HOW WILL YOU COMMUNICATE IT?

A big part of being a successful communicator requires that a musician is able to convey, through sound, many modes of expression, including: calm, reflection, excitement, sadness, beauty, chaos, story, etc. Let your students know that communicating those elements in music is largely identical to what an actor has to do when they project a wide variety of emotions through their voice, face, and body movement.

With that in mind, students must always ask themselves: what is the composer saying and how can I best communicate it to an audience in my own voice? Of course, that is just the starting point. To begin, the student must first, through careful score study and analysis, start to craft an aural image in their mind of the sounds they wish to produce at their instrument. Only after an aural image starts to take shape should practicing commence in earnest, with the student continually working to make sure that the music they are producing is a good marriage of their interpretation and the composer's intent.

Exercise: Ask your student what they feel the specific intent of a section should be? Perhaps they will point out a particular syncopation that they feel needs to be highlighted, or that a motor rhythm should portray a heightened sense of driving, relentless forward motion, or that they detect in the music a feeling of anticipation that needs to be brought out. Once a student determines a musical intention through their score study, they should indicate that intent by writing it down in the exact place it belongs in the score. They should then continue to another section and write in more comments in this manner until the whole piece has been finished. Next, those written musical intentions must be practiced carefully into the music itself on a daily basis so they will become secure and, later, clearly projected during performance.

As things become solid, the student should practice playing through their pieces as if they were in performance. This can be very tiring, which is why this necessary step is often neglected or avoided altogether. It is crucial here that your students receive frequent feedback regarding the level to which they are succeeding in communicating their musical ideas. This can be achieved from multiple sources: recording devices, fellow musicians, you (their teacher), and by playing in competitions where written critiques are provided. It is vitally important that the student has thought about their interpretation as it correlates to the musical intent of the composer in each section and piece. As students will find out, however, defining a musical purpose and being able to project it through an instrument are two very different things. Prompt your students to ask, "This is the musical intention I wanted to project to the listener, did it come across to you?" By being specific in this way, students will gain a better awareness of just what levels they must achieve for their musical purposes to be clearly felt by an audience.

PHILOSOPHY OF TRANSMITTING IDEAS AND EMOTION

Once a student has defined a certain idea, emotion, or quality they wish to express to their audience in a particular measure or section of music, they must be able to transmit it. The next question for most students becomes, how should *they feel* while performing to make a particular emotion become manifest through sound? Does a musician have to feel an emotion to project it well? Answers will, obviously, vary on this.

In my experience as a performer, however, expressing an emotion or musical idea is best done without the need to actually "experience" or "feel" it at the moment of performance. Instead, I prefer to stay focused on the physical act of *how* I am going to generate that emotion or idea. That was not always the case: as a student, I often experienced the negative effects of getting caught up in "feeling" swirling, yet undefined emotions during my performances; most of the time that only worked to derail memorization or caused me to lose some technical control, and rarely worked to my benefit.

FEELING EMOTION VS. KNOWING HOW TO PORTRAY THE EMOTION

Let's explore this a bit more…because you may be thinking, "How can he propose playing a performance without feeling emotion?" It may have surprised you when I stated earlier that students do not have to "feel" much at all from an emotional standpoint to successfully project a powerful and emotion-laden musical idea. My students almost always become more expressive when they learn to translate an emotion they wish to project into physical gesture at the keyboard and leave the actual "feeling" part out. By doing so, they become adept in expressing themselves at their instrument by knowing precisely which physical gestures are needed for projecting any one musical intention and then doing so in the right place. Remember, the classical actor does not have to feel the emotion behind the blood-curdling scream they must produce convincingly night after night in a play. Instead, they render the scream effectively through the physical knowledge of "how" to make their voice sound that way at that exact moment and the energy needed to project it into the theater. (This philosophy differs from "method acting" in which the actor feels the actual emotion during the scream, an exhausting and draining style that, if adopted by musicians, does not lend itself to maintaining fine motor control when playing an instrument.) In essence, you want your student to understand that successful communication is being able to help an *audience* to feel an emotion. The student, as performer, doesn't need to.

There's an important point to make in all of this: once a student can clearly define what they have to do physically to make a certain musical effect take place, such as increase the tempo or dynamic level, it becomes much easier to execute and, consequently, for the idea to be communicated. The needed physical gestures should then become the primary focus. I have found that simplifying the process works best. Clear, simple physical directives—previously well-established through practice—make performing under pressure a much easier task and provide a greater chance for successful communication.

Exercise: Start by asking your students to try to describe what must be done *physically* (not emotionally) at the keyboard in order to express, for example, simplicity, sweetness, or excitement; then ask them to demonstrate at the keyboard. They may pick excitement. Ideally (and with some well-directed questions), the student might go on to describe the exact process to achieve that emotion (i.e., the passage should be played fast and loud, so increase the dynamic level to create a crescendo, and add an accelerando). You might reply to your student, "Great, that's a good blueprint! Are there any specific emotions *you* need to feel to achieve this goal? Or could the excitement you want to convey to an audience be achieved by focusing only on what you have to do physically to make it manifest, such as by playing increasingly louder and faster?" You could also ask, in a different way, "If you were to feel an emotion while performing this passage, what, exactly, would it be—an increase in happiness, fear, panic, or excitement? If so, how would those feelings be beneficial? Might those feelings (and adrenaline) contribute to a loss of control at the instrument rather than benefiting your playing? Wouldn't it be exhausting as a performer to constantly experience a wide range of emotions over the course of a performance? Would that be a sustainable method for you?"

CONTEXTUALIZING COMMUNICATION (RHETORICAL) ELEMENTS USED IN MUSIC

Exercise: Hopefully, your students will now begin seeing themselves as purposeful communicators—musicians with something specific to say through a process they had previously planned, thought out, and practiced. To further help students toward this goal, ask them to name some familiar elements that are crucial to musical expression, such as dynamics, articulations, phrasing, rubato, nuance, etc. In order to maximize the potential effectiveness of any one of those elements, students will have to make sure each has a purpose and context. (As we know, composers' markings have much thought behind them as well.) Here are two short examples to more fully illustrate what I mean:

Old way: A student plays an indicated crescendo in a score. They blindly increase the dynamics without any concept of how this crescendo is a part of a larger picture or any sense of its context within a section, movement, or piece. Without this sort of context, a performer is basically just "painting by number," with no sense of the image they ultimately will render. That's no way to communicate effectively.

New way: When your student spots that crescendo in the score, they look at it in the way a writer would when choosing to make a specific point. First, the crescendo itself must be played absolutely clearly—executed in a way so that there is no question what it is—with an exact beginning, middle, and end. Second, and even more important, the context of the crescendo must be gleaned from what *surrounds* it. By doing this, the student will have a better idea of how the crescendo will fit with the music around it. For example, a crescendo following a very soft section would not have to have a dramatic increase in volume in order to convey the sense of getting louder. In addition, the student needs to consider what dynamic the crescendo begins and ends on and how long a distance it spans in order to pace it accordingly.

RHETORICAL DEVICES IN SPEECH CAN ALSO BE USED IN MUSIC

Rhetoric is the art of communicating effectively through speech. For the spoken and written word, rhetorical devices are numerous, including: allusion (an indirect reference), analogy (this corresponds or functions like that), antithesis (the opposite of something), epithet (a word or phrase that describes a characteristic of someone), hyperbole (exaggerations that aren't literal), simile (majestic as an eagle), etc. To be sure, the rhetorical devices in the language of music are not as specific as those in spoken and written language. But the rhetorical devices shared by music and word can be explored as close equivalents, and I think they should be considered to help the student expand their expressive possibilities.

Many pieces of music contain recurring themes or phrases, either repeated identically or varied a bit as the music progresses. How might a performer play these phrases in a way that not only helps the listener recall that they have heard them before, but sustains their interest throughout the piece? Could the performer play a theme or phrase a bit more emphatically (increasing the dynamics or changing the tempo) to make a point each time its variant occurs? This might be thought of as something akin to the use of allusion. This is not unlike what a good speaker might do, repeat the same (or like) phrase differently the second time, perhaps more emphatically, for emphasis and to maintain the listeners' attention.

What about the idea of hyperbole or exaggeration? You may have once said to a student something like, "You need to play this section like a thundering freight train!" Well, you were using hyperbole (built into a simile). The student won't ever actually be nearly as loud as a freight train—but you made an effective pedagogical point. (And I bet that the student will probably always "thunder" as loudly as they can in that passage after hearing your suggestion.) Could you also teach these rhetorical connections for students to create and use in their own playing to increase their expressiveness? I believe hyperbole (among many other rhetorical devices) is an important concept for artists to keep in mind and employ in their music-making. For example, don't we usually need to exaggerate our musical ideas in order for the audience to clearly hear them? Pianissimos really need to whisper like soft breezes and fortissimos need to thunder, well, like a freight train. And, to use an example from another art field, consider what stage makeup on an actor looks like up close—how overdone and exaggerated it has to be in order to be effective at a distance. The actor uses hyperbole, in multiple forms—not just in appearance, but in word and movement as well.

We now see that rhetorical elements in speech have parallels in music and should be considered as part of the expressive arsenal of any musician. The teacher can think creatively along these lines to help their students apply these parallels. I often examine the connections between speech and music because of how it sparks the imagination and benefits my playing.

Recall listening to a convincing and captivating speaker, perhaps at a past commencement or political rally. Weren't many of the expressive devices the speaker used similar, if not directly analogous, to those a good musician regularly employs in performance? These spoken devices include dynamics, accents, rubato, pauses, crescendos, diminuendos, staccato, legato, and pacing—all the same elements we use as musicians! In addition, both language and music use elements such as clarity, expression, train of thought, context, clear delivery, ability to project, dramatization, and so on. All of those elements, too, can be used to help your students become more effective and expressive "speakers" through their instruments. To help students understand and learn from the language/music connection more fully, encourage them to step outside the field of music and observe rhetorical elements at work in other areas, such as their schools' theater productions or debate competitions. Observing similar skills at work in another discipline can help improve their use within one's own discipline. This idea is integral to this book, so let's explore further!

OBSERVE RHETORICAL ELEMENTS AND DEVICES IN ACTION IN DIFFERENT DISCIPLINES

To broaden a student's understanding of the importance and power of good communication skills, encourage them to identify shared rhetorical devices found in disciplines like stage acting, speech-making, and music performance, using the musical devices mentioned in the paragraph above (such as dynamics, pauses, rubato, etc.). Each discipline naturally uses those rhetorical devices a little differently. It is through this diversity of use that your students gain deeper insight into, and obtain a more comprehensive understanding of, the rhetorical devices themselves. This process of scrutinizing like skills at work in other disciplines can provide your students with more ideas to use in their own music-making.

Advanced exercise: Perhaps the best source to use for this observational process is YouTube. There, students will have virtually an unlimited supply of acting, news anchor, speech-making, and music performance clips to view rhetorical elements in action. Ask your students to make sure the clips they are going to study are good examples (reputable news stations, political debates, well-known artists) that are visually and audibly clear and demonstrate a variety of rhetorical devices. Students will soon notice the universality of shared rhetorical devices when they see how pauses, gesture, volume change, speeding up, slowing down, etc., are all part of the effective communicator's toolkit, no matter the medium. Those devices are the very elements students use in their playing each day, and they should be thought about and practiced for the student to develop them to their fullest potential.

As your students watch various YouTube clips as outside lesson assignments, ask them to pay particular attention to the degree to which rhetorical elements are employed and effective, even when they are not so obvious. For example, assign them to identify places where the use of the pause (the rest or breath in music) or change of pace in a speech (rubato, accelerando, or ritard) is very slight. Minimal, highly nuanced rhetorical devices can be very effective in music and in speech—the listener feels the intent of them, but is often unaware of them.

Ask your students to be especially attentive to how effective even the most minimal use of a rhetorical device can be. Connect each expressive, spoken device to its parallel in music and then have them practice applying minimal change in the playing. For example, how slight can a ritard be, yet still be effective? You can also help direct your students' attention by asking questions like the following: how much do the same rhetorical devices vary between different people and why might they have been employed? How do they all contribute to clarity of communicating a thought, idea, or emotion? How might you use similar devices in music and speech to your advantage?

When a writer or speaker has a point to make, she is, in essence, *selling* the idea through her ability to persuade with the use of well-chosen words, clarity of purpose, and a delivery that maximizes expression and drama. A performer's musical idea may be "sold" to an audience in much the same way; through the power of its delivery, emotional content, clarity, and conviction.

MODES OF EXPRESSION

The musician who makes the connection between the language of words and the language of music will find that *one provides insights into the other.* This is the beauty of intersectionality and the cross-training concept. For example, if a speaker wishes to emphasize a particular point in speech she might say something louder, enunciate more emphatically, or slow down to make sure that it is clearly heard and understood. In the same way, when a musician wishes to make a point, such as letting the listener know the importance of a small change in a returning melody or a change of modality, they might "enunciate" it more by voicing the melody out more or lingering a bit on the part that changed.

It must be said that good communication first requires, above all, a clear understanding of what the message is and how it is going to be delivered. This should all be fully determined beforehand, not in the moment. If one struggles with making a musical point during a performance, it is usually because the idea itself has not yet come into focus—and thus cannot be articulated clearly.

COMMUNICATION EXERCISES USING SPEECH AND WRITTEN WORD

1. SPEECH

Try asking your students to practice dramatizing a few made-up sentences to help them increase the expressive power in their music. Invite them to pretend they are stage actors projecting emotion clearly throughout the theater. Make up fun sentences that ooze drama and emotion, such as: "You will go over the falls if you swim any closer!" or "You'll never get away with this—I will track you to the ends of the earth!" or "I know the answer you have spent your life seeking... (long pause), your brother is alive and well in Sweden." Ask your student to vary their delivery of these phrases by changing tempos, dynamics, articulations, pacing, intensity, etc. Try different combinations with friends so there can be some feedback. First, try saying (delivering) the example phrases with no emotion; then, again, this time packed full of emotion. This exercise can give students a taste of some of the devices used in communicating effectively. And, at the same time, it may reward the students with further insights into becoming better communicators on their instruments.

2. WRITTEN WORD

Ask your student to write a short sales pitch on why their particular talents are best-suited to a certain job (they can make one up). Is it concise, compelling, clear, and correct, with no embellishments? In their written pitch, have them mark above the corresponding words all the expressive devices they will be using, such as pauses, slowing down, speeding up, whispering, crescendos, etc. Make sure they keep the connections to music in mind. When they have finished marking their script, ask your student to try giving their pitch as if an important job depended upon it. Make sure to follow along on a separate copy to see how well the student is following their own marks of expression. Can marks of expression be overdone? Yes— things can become comically over-emphasized. If this happens, help your student establish where they might tone things down; help them establish parameters. And, as always, make the connection to music, which will be our next step.

APPLICATION TO MUSIC

Once students complete the two exercises above, have them apply the ideas they have learned about effective communication in speech and word to a piece of music they are currently working on. Rhetorical elements can be indicated by adding additional, supportive comments to the composer's expressive indications in the score. These could include short descriptions about what the student believes the over-all musical objective might be: a long pause here, a gigantic forte there; stretch these three notes; over-voice the melody in this section; make this phrase sound like floating mist; make this accompaniment sound like a monotonous drone here, etc.

Next, ask your student to practice expressing those rhetorical markings in their playing during the week following their lesson. Then, at their next lesson, you can determine whether or not their musical ideas are clear and unmistakable, or at least leaning in that direction. Has your student's playing become more communicative, expressive, or emotionally charged as a result of your teaching the connection between the spoken/written word and music?

GOOD COMMUNICATION REQUIRES ENERGY

Energy is certainly needed to communicate well! Make sure your students know to make this element a priority in all communication—and, of course, in performance. Encourage students to infuse all communication with energy, be it music or word. Energy isn't just reflected through playing or speaking frenetically, loudly, or quickly. It can also be conveyed through intensity of delivery or a sense of highly charged meaning. However energy is utilized, the use of this important ingredient can be very effective in delivering a message.

Exercise: Ask the student to try to project a sense of energy in their playing. What might that sound like? Hint: clarity, control, and consistency all play a big role in projecting energy. What would it take to infuse that quality into their playing? Hint: work on focus. Does it mean that every element, no matter what it is, must be very clearly projected? Ideally, yes; it can't be over-stated that energy is certainly part of effective projection. Ultimately, there should be no question on the receivers' (audience) side as to what was intended by the sender.

III. PIVOT CHORD
Prepare to Transpose the Skill to a Non-Music Application

Now that your students have been introduced to the idea of communication (rhetoric) as a universal skill and have applied it in their music, ask them to apply the skill to non-music applications. There is a whole new range of benefits that come with this step! I need to reinforce again: Just as transposition helps to develop a melody, transposition (transference) of a universal skill—using it outside the field of music—helps to develop that skill even more. This act of transference, then, functions like cross-training by "circling back" to strengthen students' use of that skill in their music-making even more. Thus, the transposed musician possesses an active toolkit of multiple, highly-developed universal skills.

THE BENEFITS OF TRANSFERENCE

As we know from experience, the vast majority of our music students (K-12 and college level) will not go on to become professional musicians, choosing instead, other professions. Those students who practiced communication skills through the medium of music and were also helped to see them as transferable are in a much better position to re-apply those skills *universally* than those who received no formal introduction to them. And, what profession doesn't count good communication as one of its most important and in-demand skills?

IV. TRANSPOSITION
Actively Transpose the Skill to a Non-Music Application

EXERCISES FOR TRANSFERENCE

Students who have learned and actively applied rhetorical (expressive) devices in their music-making may now be in a better position to use them in non-music applications—specifically, through the medium for which they were initially used: language. Even though spoken language (usually) starts earlier than playing an instrument, music can certainly inform and benefit the student in the use of more expressive speaking skills. Make sure your students understand the importance of practicing good communication skills and how doing so can benefit almost every facet of life. Not only is developing this skill important, it can be an invigorating and fun life-long journey. Each of your students will have multiple instances where they can begin to transfer their well-learned communication skills from music to language and writing, such as in classes at school, at their part-time jobs, and in their everyday lives.

To begin this transference exercise, suggest to your students that they apply the "four Cs" they learned first in the music application—concise, compelling, clear, and correct—to a fun, easy-to-use play-acting exercise that can be used for making clear and constructive verbal critiques in their performance classes. It's an approach I use in my piano performance classes to help students feel less awkward or reticent about commenting critically on each other's performances. It frees them up dramatically and, consequently, increases their ability to pinpoint issues. I found it worked so well that I documented this approach in an article, "The Piano Performance Class as Theater: A Dramatized Interactive Class with Informative Role-Playing."[5] Using this approach, students make up and play-act oddball characters who comment upon each other's performances in piano class. These exercises allow students to practice the transference of their music communication skills to speech—in a fun, active-learning environment. In these exercises, ask your students to practice using one of the "four Cs" at a time. The point of these following exercises is the clarity and effective use of verbal communication through critiques, not the actual music performance itself. They might unfold like this:

1. Ask your students to be as **concise** as possible in their comments about a fellow student's performance. Taisha has decided to play a character she has developed, named Mrs. Tothepoint. That character brags about being able to make her points in sometimes three or fewer words. After hearing a fellow student finish a Scarlatti Sonata, Mrs. Tothepoint offered her comments in quick, clipped tones: "Too fast, not clean enough, not even enough." Everyone laughed, as did the student at the piano. Yet, all agreed that she was right on target with her points—and very succinct. Her verbal communication was successful. Another student, playing a character called Dr. Presto, offered suggestions as to how the Scarlatti performer could remedy those same issues. Dr. Presto was able to use concise language to articulate three helpful practice tips in a short space of time, including: "Focus on slow practice, always keep fingers even, and increase speed slowly for continued control." In both character sketches, the play-acting allowed the students to 1.) lose their fear of

talking in a group setting and 2.) drop their concerns about criticizing others' performances. They also better-assimilated the goal of the exercise when in character—communicating concisely and to the point.

2. After hearing another student play a Chopin Waltz, students in the performance class were asked to make a **compelling** argument for why they may have liked or disliked the interpretation—and, of course, to do so in character. One student, in a character named Herr Touchtone, made a persuasive argument that the slower-than-marked tempo and high degree of lyricism was just as valid as the faster, more commonly taken tempo. In fact, he said, because it was slower, the listener would hear more expressive elements and would find it more engaging. Using rhetorical devices that had parallels to those in music performance, including speaking with a wide range of dynamics, inflections, and numerous pregnant pauses, he convincingly made his argument. For contrast, his teacher asked him to repeat a few sentences from the beginning of his argument, but this time using a quasi-monotone. The difference was striking: the same words just did not seem nearly as convincing as they did the first time. The class knew, at once, why the teacher had asked Herr Touchtone to modify his delivery in such a way—good verbal communication is very dependent upon elements of expression; just as in music.

3. With another performance, ask your students to make **clarity** their main objective when critiquing the next pianist.

Remind them to be mindful of their word choices, avoiding poorly chosen words or points that may not be clear. Also remind them to recall what they learned in their lessons about applying this same step in their music performance: will there be any question in the listeners' minds as to what is being expressed when you play? You call on one student, play-acting Mr. Largoissimo, who has had difficulty being clear in his past critiques of fellow studio mates' performances, to critique Sarah's performance of one of Ginastera's *Danzas Argentinas*. This time, you ask him to take a little more time to think through what he wants to say *before* starting to comment. In fact, you say with a big smile, it's required! After thinking for about 30 seconds after Sarah had finished playing, Mr. Largoissimo commented that he felt that the performance had great energy and excitement. He said the success of those elements came from the clarity of the rhythms and steadiness of the tempo Sarah took. You tell him that his critique was much more clear this time than in the past and ask him what changed this time. He replied that he felt it was mainly about taking more time to think—and trying to genuinely notice and articulate his own feelings.

4. Finally, you ask your students to discuss amongst themselves the use of self-critique (a form of inner communication) to ensure that they are **correct** in the assessments of their *own* playing. How might use of rhetorical devices such as simile, metaphor, and hyperbole in self-assessment talk be either beneficial or harmful? Ask a few questions to get them started: If someone were to hear you speaking to yourself,

what might it sound like; how might you convey a needed concern or self-critique? What tone would you take; would you be harsh, or more kind and understanding? How clear would the message be?

The use of the four "Cs" in this "performance class as theater" session was just a convenient starting point to use as a possible example. You can create any number of speaking or writing exercises for your students to use as part of introducing the idea of transference after they have become comfortable applying rhetorical elements in their playing. For example, you might ask your students how they might apply their new speaking skills in a part-time job, in a school book report, or persuading someone in a class discussion? The main idea here is to get them thinking about the universality of skilled communication and how they can exercise it to its fullest potential.

V. RECAP
Revisit the Skill in Music

This chapter was intended to help music teachers with ideas that can benefit their students to become more effective communicators at their instrument. At the same time, the idea of transference was an equally important part of the lesson in which communication was related to both music and to speech/written word. In my experience, exercising a particular skill in more than one discipline has provided me greater insights and ability into using the skill than if I had applied it solely in music. And, it often circles back to further benefit the original application—in this case, music. For example, after practicing speaking through a paper in preparation for a presentation at a major conference, I became even more conscious of how to more effectively use elements of rhetoric in my music, making better use of pause, buildup, inflection, and clarity of intent. I learned to apply a better sense of pacing to my performances as well.

As I have mentioned before, the transference of any universal skill to another discipline is *not* something that will occur automatically with a majority of your students. Transference is a concept that music teachers should constantly encourage their students to think about, engage in, and apply on their own time. Teaching transference is especially important and valid for every music teacher who feels that the purpose of the music lesson should be broadened to more comprehensively help their students in both music and in life.

VI. QUESTIONS FOR REFLECTION

1. How have the ideas in this chapter about developing communication skills in music and in speech/writing changed your students' way of practicing and expressing themselves?

2. Are they more expressive and effective in communicating a message, whether in the medium of music or of language?

3. Are your students more motivated to work on improving their levels of communication (expression) and make it a more important part of every practice session, now that they see the connections between verbal and musical expression?

4. Has identifying and using specific rhetorical elements in music given your students greater expressive possibilities?

5. How has thinking about effective communication in other disciplines (speaking, writing, and acting) helped your students' effectiveness in communicating through music? Vice versa?

6. Did the students who took part in the "performance class as theater" exercise learn to better "dramatize" their musical performances? To communicate more effectively?

VII. SUGGESTED READING

Barker, Alan. *Improve Your Communication Skills* 4th ed. London, UK: Kogan Page, 2016.

Bhatara, Anjali, Petri Laukka, and Daniel J. Levitin. *Expressions of Emotion in Music and Vocal Communication*. Meda, SA: *Frontiers in Psychology*, 2007-2014. (A compilation of journal articles from *Frontiers in Psychology*.)

Davis, Martha, Patrick Fanning, and Matthew McKay. *Messages: The Communication Skills Book* 3rd ed. Oakland, CA: New Harbinger Publications, Inc., 2009.

Farnsworth, Ward. *Farnsworth's Classical English Rhetoric.* Boston, MA: David R. Godine Publishing, 2010.

Forsyth, Mark. *The Elements of Eloquence, Secrets of the Perfect Turn of Phrase.* New York, NY: The Berkley Publishing Group, 2013.

Kortepeter, Paul. *Writing and Rhetoric Book 3: Narrative II.* Camp Hill, PA: Classical Academic Press, 2014.

Luntz, Frank. *Words That Work: It's Not What You Say, It's What People Hear.* New York, NY: Hyperion, 2007.

MacDonald, Raymond and David J. Hargreaves. *Musical Communication.* Oxford, UK: Oxford University Press, 2005.

Maxwell, John, C., *Everyone Communicates, Few Connect: What the Most Effective People Do Differently.* Nashville, TN: Thomas Nelson, Inc., 2010.

VIII. REFERENCES

1. John C. Maxwell, *Everyone Communicates, Few Connect* (Nashville, TN: Thomas Nelson, Inc., 2010), 34.
2. Chuck Garcia, *A Climb to the Top* (Charleston, SC: Advantage, 2016), 129.
3. John C. Maxwell, ibid, 11.
4. Richard Worth, *Communication Skills* (Chicago, IL: New England Associates/Ferguson Publishing Co., 2004), 19.
5. Dylan Savage, "The Piano Performance Class as Theater: A Dramatized Interactive Class with Informative Role-Playing." *Clavier Companion* 7, No. 3 (May/June 2015): 56-8.

IX. NOTES

CHAPTER 6

COLLABORATION

"Jazz urges you to accept the decisions of others."
—Wynton Marsalis.[1]

"One way to build team spirit in your team members is to show
them how what they accomplish contributes to the bottom line."
—Arthur R. Pell.[2]

"Collaboration drives creativity because innovation always
emerges from a series of sparks—never a single flash of insight."
—Keith Sawyer.[3]

"Communication: The lifeblood of team success."
—Arthur R. Pell.[4]

I. SKILL IMPORTANCE, CONTEXT, DEFINITION, AND BREAKDOWN

SKILL IMPORTANCE

We often hear about the importance of developing collaborative skills—the ones that allow us to work well with others. Many have found that collaborative skills are not always easy to apply, due in part to the many challenging differences in individual personalities. As musicians, it's no secret that we spend a great deal of time in collaborative settings. Yet how prepared are young musicians when they sit down in their first string quartet, piano trio, or band rehearsal? How many musicians struggle to surmount the interpersonal and teamwork challenges of working closely together in ensembles? Are they given techniques for collaborative etiquette, or pointers that go beyond the cursory?

This chapter addresses these questions by laying out some ideas about formal instruction in the collaborative process. Becoming an excellent collaborator can have a positive impact on a music career. For example, the musician who demonstrates good collaborative skills as a substitute player is more likely to be called back or perhaps recommended for an audition with the ensemble if a position comes open. That's because most people prefer to work with folks who get along and who contribute well. Also, the ensemble that works well together will most likely play better as a group—and that surely has an impact upon the success of the ensemble. Yet, in my experience, many music students exhibit limited collaborative ability and have to fend for themselves through trial and error, having never been taught a systematic approach to learning collaborative skills.

Additionally, communication skills learned in the previous chapter (clarity, conciseness, etc.) will be beneficial in any situation where collaboration is necessary.

SKILL CONTEXT

Here lies a great opportunity for us as music teachers: why not help our students by training them with a basic set of rules on collaboration? Then, after giving students a formalized approach to collaboration as it applies to music, help them see that the benefits extend not only to music but to all of life as well. Think of learning a basic set of collaborative steps in the same vein as parents teaching their children codes of conduct and manners. In both instances, they are necessary to successfully navigate interactions with people—and they are fairly similar, too!

For musicians, the ability to collaborate well means being able to interact diplomatically with fellow musicians through speech *and* music in a way that allows for honest and full discourse. In my view, the foundation of good collaborative qualities must include empathy, a desire to help, patience, an overriding sense of goodwill, and, yes, forgiveness. With those qualities, mountains can be moved! Yet, when have we last seen all those at work in a music ensemble? Because of the inherent tendency for group dynamics to skitter off balance, the music ensemble presents very specific and significant challenges for the unprepared. Chief among those challenges is the vulnerability issue: our playing, with all its strengths and weaknesses, is on full display...both to our fellow players and to an audience. Add in the amount of time, effort, and struggle each musician has put into arriving at the point where they are and there is real potential for some emotional miscues and misfires. Group dynamics can be quite a minefield to navigate for those who haven't given much thought or practice to the basic principles of collaboration.

Working in a group includes having to solve a constant flow of musical and technical issues. That process, of course, involves having these issues pointed out—usually by someone else, such as the conductor, section leader, or stand partner. In other words, the music ensemble is a place where students can feel quite vulnerable; a place where emotions can run high if people conduct themselves undiplomatically. How can students learn to be more constructive in their comments without coming across as critical or insensitive? With no codes of conduct to guide them while collaborating, misunderstandings can occur and multiply—all of which can be quite problematic.

So, why expect students to reinvent the wheel by leaving the collaborative process up to them to learn and navigate? Students should be taught systematic collaborative skills early on, to take the guesswork out of operating successfully in an entity many instrumental and vocal students engage in daily—the ensemble. This chapter is dedicated to side-stepping that trial and error process by offering a series of steps I have used for years in my studio and in my ensemble classes. First, let's get on the same page regarding what collaboration generally is taken to mean.

SKILL DEFINITION

Most definitions of collaboration contain this basic statement: the ability of individuals to work together toward a common goal or purpose. Wow, how disarmingly simple (yet sometimes, how difficult to accomplish!).

SKILL BREAKDOWN

For years, I have taught a series of collaborative steps to my music students, based on a list used by the University of Strathclyde in Glasgow, Scotland.[5] Even though the list was originally meant for use in non-music disciplines, I found it ideally-suited for musicians as well. Here is a brief summary of that list:

1. "The ability to work with others on a common task."[6]
2. "Taking actions which respect the needs and contributions of others."[7]
3. "Contributing to and accepting consensus."[8]
4. "Negotiating a win-win situation to achieve the objectives of the team."[9]

Now let's apply these steps to collaborating with fellow musicians.

II. TONIC KEY
Learn to Apply the Skill to Music

FOUR KEYS OF GOOD COLLABORATION AND TEAMWORK SKILLS

1. HAVING THE ABILITY TO WORK WITH OTHERS IN AN ENSEMBLE.

I always start with this statement as the opening description of collaboration to my students. I ask them to think about how they might apply it to issues they have faced while collaborating in the past: were there difficulties with fellow players, and what was done to help mitigate issues, if anything? What role did tempers play; was it difficult to be diplomatic? What role did my student play in making teamwork in the group or ensemble more positive or negative? I follow up by asking the student what the word "ability" means in this context. To help students with this question, I mention that "ability" in the ensemble setting can mean many things: listening well, controlling counter-productive knee-jerk reactions or emotions, nurturing others, leading by example, exhibiting empathy, being positive, showing respect, engaging diplomacy, and a whole host of other beneficial attributes—many of which may need to be thought about and worked upon.

2. TAKING ACTIONS THAT RESPECT THE NEEDS AND CONTRIBUTIONS OF OTHERS IN THEIR GROUP.

I ask my students to reflect on this statement before I help them zero in more on what this might mean. The word "respecting" in this context has many applications, such as encouraging a weaker player or giving a stand-mate reassurance during a trying moment in a rehearsal. Respecting the contributions of others can mean genuinely complimenting someone when it is clearly due, not diffusing an accomplishment by ignoring it or minimizing it in some way. Respect of another's contribution can also be shown by reflecting it through one's playing. For example: after hearing a particularly beautiful turn of a phrase by another ensemble member, others could make the choice to play it in a like manner.

3. CONTRIBUTING TO AND ACCEPTING THE CONSENSUS OF YOUR FELLOW MUSICIANS.

Giving 100% to an interpretation that one doesn't completely agree with is understandably difficult. In the best of circumstances, an interpretation is developed enthusiastically by the *whole* group through consensus. But what if the conductor or section leader has determined that a piece of music is going to be interpreted in a particular way and it's an approach your student just does not agree with at all? This is exactly the time when the student has to graciously accept the decision and then throw themselves into making manifest the interpretation they don't agree with. Good teamwork requires just that kind of effort and commitment. Alert your students to the fact that this step may require practice and personal development. Oftentimes, embracing an interpretation that one doesn't initially agree upon can later lead to new discoveries and perhaps even spur a surprising about-face.

4. NEGOTIATING A WIN-WIN SITUATION TO ACHIEVE THE OBJECTIVES OF YOUR ENSEMBLE.

This can mean that discussion, bargaining, and perhaps some concessions are necessary for an ensemble to reach a unified interpretation: where (almost) everyone gets something they want. That is negotiation. This concept of a win-win solution to a group dispute may be a new concept altogether for some, especially when it applies to music. It especially benefits situations in which there are strong and disparate notions on how a piece of music should go. Reiterate to your students that playing well together requires embracing a common goal or interpretation—and that getting everyone to that point may require some negotiation. In an ensemble situation where multiple perspectives exist regarding how a section or piece should be played, it is important to discuss all the possibilities. This might include trying them, negotiating, and blending points of view to ultimately achieve an interpretation all can live with.

These four keys provide a good starting place for students in understanding the definition and scope of collaboration. I like that they originated from a business perspective—it demonstrates how collaboration, and the other skills in this book, are truly universal. Additionally, it encourages students to think about how these skills might be applied across disciplines. As I have mentioned, the idea of skill transference is central to this book because it gives the student a much broader range of use for each skill—something from which they will most definitely benefit.

ENCOURAGE CONVERSATIONS ABOUT COLLABORATION

Even after your students start learning and using some of the basic collaboration skills found in this chapter, continue to keep conversations going with your students about collaboration. You might ask questions such as: in the ensemble in which you play, what's a common challenge in your section? Is there more than one issue?

Do you hear consensus or division in the sound? What does working "together" mean to you? How might you better respect the needs and contributions of others? What could be meant by "negotiating" a win-win situation in a rehearsal? Encourage discussion and remind students to listen to one another, even if they don't agree.

Once your students understand the basic idea and function of the four keys listed above and have discussed their application in the music ensemble, they may be interested to learn a little more detail to help them become more accomplished collaborators.

FURTHER ASPECTS OF COLLABORATION

If you think your students would benefit from some additional, more nuanced steps to the original four collaborative keys that were just covered, Strathclyde University has an extended list with further suggestions on collaboration:

1. "GIVE AND RECEIVE FEEDBACK FROM PEERS OR OTHER TEAM MEMBERS IN ORDER TO PERFORM THE TASK."[10]

I really like this suggestion and always encourage my students to be open to receiving feedback from their peers. Even if they do not always agree with the feedback they receive, there is often something of merit to consider. If they are asked to provide feedback, they should consider it an honor and do so honestly, thoughtfully, and respectfully.

2. "SHARE CREDIT FOR GOOD IDEAS WITH OTHERS."[11]

Great advice! No one likes to hear someone bragging about how great their idea was or trying to take full credit for one that was not entirely theirs. I always mentor students to be humble in accounting for their accomplishments and to give others credit along the way.

3. "ACKNOWLEDGE OTHERS' SKILL, EXPERIENCE, CREATIVITY, AND CONTRIBUTIONS."[12]

When students take this point to heart, it helps build their sense of humility and provides them great opportunities to learn by recognizing and appreciating accomplishments of others. When your student is aware of and acknowledges another team-member's contributions, they are practicing good collaboration skills.

4. "LISTEN TO AND ACKNOWLEDGE THE FEELING, CONCERNS, OPINIONS, AND IDEAS OF OTHERS."[13]

People like to know they have been heard. One can disagree with an idea or interpretation while at the same time acknowledging they heard and understood what was being said or played. Encourage students to become good, empathetic listeners, both while performing and while discussing concerns in their ensembles. After acknowledging an idea, even if it doesn't seem to be a good one, adding to it or making a change will be much easier and more comfortable for all involved.

5. "EXPAND ON THE IDEA OF A PEER OR TEAM MEMBER."[14]

When an idea is being discussed, adding to it in a positive and supportive way shows engagement and interest toward a common goal. In a music ensemble, this point might take the form of a response such as, "I loved your description of how we could get this passage to sound lighter and freer. It might also help to try playing the notes with a little more detached articulation. Shall we try that?"

6. "STATE PERSONAL OPINIONS AND AREAS OF DISAGREEMENT TACTFULLY."[15]

Make sure your students understand the power of diplomacy. Instead of saying, "You are totally not following the composer's directions"—which could make anyone defensive—try saying, "Help us understand better why you think it should be interpreted in that manner" or "Could we try it another way and then discuss the two versions?" A great starting point is to ask your students how *they* would like to be spoken to and tell them to always think before speaking and to be polite.

7. "LISTEN PATIENTLY TO OTHERS IN CONFLICT SITUATIONS."[16]

This suggestion is related to number four above. What musician hasn't been in a conflict-type situation from time to time? It can easily occur in a chamber ensemble when there are many concerns to be voiced. Taking time to patiently and respectfully hear someone's concerns goes a long way toward keeping conflicts from escalating.

8. "DEFINE PROBLEMS IN A NON-THREATENING MANNER."[17]

This largely involves not making statements that blatantly assign blame to someone such as: "It's your fault" or "You always miss that entrance." Instead say, "Could we try that again? And this time, let's all pay special attention to coming in together on beat two of the second measure."

9. "SUPPORT GROUP DECISIONS EVEN IF NOT IN TOTAL AGREEMENT."[18]

Invariably, an ensemble without a conductor has to come to a consensus on a particular way of playing something with a particular character or in a specific tempo. Not everyone will agree. In these instances, it is usually best to allow a democratic majority to hold sway.

FINDING THE POSITIVE

Finally, I ask my students to think about how they might extract more fun and joy from their collaborative experiences. At times, this goal may seem like a stretch to accomplish, especially when an ensemble performance may not have gone well or your student didn't feel they played their best. However, even if things don't go well, there can be positives to extract from the experience. Remind your student to try to focus on the parts of a performance which they felt good about—maybe it was simply the act of playing with others. Have them try to identify a positive takeaway from the performance instead of fixating on the negative parts and suffering the effects. Then, acknowledge the changes that need to be made and resolve to deal with them thoughtfully and effectively during the next rehearsal or practice session.

III. PIVOT CHORD
Prepare to Transpose the Skill to a Non-Music Application

We know that many of our music students are already working in non-music collaborative settings, either at their schools or part-time jobs. By giving your students specific instruction on these universal skill applications in the music lesson and then, through transference, leading them to apply those skills in life, you provide them with beneficial and powerful tools they will use forever, regardless of what career they choose. By doing this, the reach of your teaching extends far beyond the boundaries of the traditional music lesson and opens up a whole new world of possibilities. This is the new and largely unexplored potential of the transposed 21st century music teacher!

When my students first come to me, they generally report that they don't *consciously* apply universal skills learned in the music lesson to life outside music. It's not that they resist doing so, it's that it usually does not occur to them—and they just haven't been encouraged to think in this way. Considering the benefits, I feel it is important for the teacher to make the connection for their students if the value of the skill in non-music applications is to be maximized. It usually doesn't take much to get a student thinking about the idea and benefits of transference. *Sometimes just introducing the idea is enough* to start your students thinking and experimenting.

The goal here is for the teacher to expand the purpose and benefits of the music lesson by including a skill transference component. Why? Your student will now be much more apt to use the critical universal skills mentioned in this book more often and consciously in all aspects of their lives. This is all the more important given that many younger students will go on to study other disciplines in college, and most of our college music students will likely not go on to be professional musicians. Further, as I have discovered on so many occasions, students who learn how to apply a skill in both music and non-music situations find that their overall ability to use that skill usually increases significantly.

TO HELP YOUR STUDENTS' PERSPECTIVE: THE IMPORTANCE OF COLLABORATION IN NON-MUSIC FIELDS

Teaching collaboration and teamwork skills to employees is something on which companies spend a great deal of money. They do so to improve the ability of their employees to work together, which then benefits productivity. Needless to say, developing collaboration skills among employees is a big challenge for businesses. Their efforts to do so clearly indicate that people often find it challenging to work well together—revealing that their collaboration skills are lacking. Your music students, on the other hand, who learned this collaboration skill early in life and practiced it often, may have a distinct advantage over the general workforce. Regardless of their ultimate career paths, your music students will always be able to use their valuable collaborative skills to great benefit, no matter what the application. And you will have done them an enormous favor just by including the transference element in the lesson.

Now that your student has applied good collaboration skills in music settings, they are ready to apply the same steps to non-music applications.

IV. TRANSPOSITION
Actively Transpose the Skill to a Non-Music Application

FOUR KEYS OF COLLABORATION AND TEAMWORK SKILLS

1. THE ABILITY TO WORK WITH OTHERS ON A COMMON TASK.

Ask your students if they can name situations where they currently have to work with others outside the field of music. What are some of the challenges that they encounter? You'll hear plenty of examples, including group school projects to part-time jobs. As in music ensembles, the ability to work with others in non-music areas requires a mix of humility, politeness, listening, contributing to a shared goal, discussion, give-and-take, and diplomacy.

Example: George, one of your students, finds himself in a school science project with five other schoolmates. Positive energy and enthusiasm abounds—yet no one wants to relinquish their personal ideas on how the project should progress. You ask him how the group might move past this impasse. If necessary, jog his memory by asking which of the four keys (found on page 160) might be helpful in this situation? Hopefully, George will remember the one which states that successful groups contribute to and accept consensus (key three). Hearing this, he remembers that being stymied is not an option and he must move forward with some plan of action. To do this, negotiation (key four), will most likely be needed to help create a path forward through the discussion, concession, and majority vote. George recalls from past music lessons what he knows about how the good of the group comes first and individual wants come second, and is convinced the students will find a process to move forward in their science project.

2. TAKING ACTIONS WHICH RESPECT THE NEEDS AND CONTRIBUTIONS OF OTHERS.

This means, in part, acting in ways that show humility and which are non-judgmental. That alone will go a long way in creating a respectful atmosphere. I find this a great place to remind students that if they treat people the way they would wish to be treated, they can't go wrong.

Example: If someone contributes an idea (to the group science project) that George thinks isn't very good, he will use the collaborative skills he learned in music study to spend a little more time reflecting on it and considering his response. Instead of saying "Oh, that's not a good idea, mine is much better, here's what we should do" he might say, "I think I have an idea which may work a little better—one you may all want to consider—and here it is."

3. CONTRIBUTING TO AND ACCEPTING THE CONSENSUS OF THE GROUP.

As mentioned above, this step requires give-and-take and a desire to work toward a common goal using a democratic process.

Example: George has played in music ensembles where he did not always agree on the decided interpretation, and yet he managed to give superb performances of his part while embracing someone else's or the group's viewpoint. You make sure to remind him of that fact and follow up by suggesting that he consciously exercise this same collaborative step in his science project application. Hearing that, George says, "Of course, it's pretty much the same thing. I don't always have to agree in order to still contribute well to this science project."

4. NEGOTIATING A WIN-WIN SITUATION TO ACHIEVE THE OBJECTIVES OF THE TEAM.

This step requires a group to embrace the philosophy of diplomacy and compromise over individual will and assertion.

Example: You ask George what he might do next. He immediately recalls, with a big smile, that he will have to introduce the idea of negotiation to his science project group as a tool to break impasses and as a process to achieve their end goal. He's convinced that this will encourage a healthy back-and-forth discourse in the team where each person in the group makes some concessions for the common good of the project. Embracing that ideal, everyone expects that they will give a little to get a little.

Another example: a musician's universal skills at work in a non-music environment.

Let's say that your former student, Midori (who has a significant music ensemble background), finds herself employed as an executive in the banking industry. Working closely with one of her teams, she immediately becomes aware that there is some dysfunction in the group's ability to collaborate. To help the situation, she recalls the information you once taught her regarding collaboration, including the benefits of skill transference. Using her collaborative skill ability, gained from years spent in music ensembles, Midori becomes instrumental in helping her colleagues at the bank begin working more constructively and efficiently toward common goals. At first, she listens a great deal and validates what she hears by replying, "I hear you saying this, am I correct?" Later, she asks questions such as, "Do you like where the team is right now and, if not, what could be done to change?" "How is the current approach working for the group?" Midori constantly exhibits all the qualities she wants the team to embody, just as she had in her music ensembles. In time, her team-mates at the bank find her unerring collaborative compass persuasive and helpful and start modifying their behavior, resulting in more productive teamwork. Seeing this result, Midori is pleased at having successfully applied a point her music teacher once made about practicing her universal skills: "Remember, what you wish to see come back to you, you must first exhibit." She has since seen many opportunities for that powerful message to be demonstrated and their positive results.

V. RECAP
Revisit the Skill in Music

Now that Midori has practiced her collaboration skills often in her banking position, she has found that they further reinforce how she uses them as a musician. Even though music does not provide her livelihood, she still plays often in the community and takes great pride in using her well-honed collaboration skills whenever needed. For example, Midori now feels far better equipped to deal with entrenched personality conflicts that exist in some of the ensembles she currently plays in because of her increased ability in diplomacy—something she would not have developed to such a level without "cross-training" (exercising) those skills in her current career.

VI. QUESTIONS FOR REFLECTION

1. Do your students notice any beneficial changes in the way they interact with others and in groups after you have coached them through steps of good collaboration?
2. Have you asked any of your students if they might feel comfortable with the idea of taking a leadership position now that they have developed some teamwork skills?
3. Do your students report feeling both more comfortable and adept at functioning in group or collaborative situations, and have their ensembles or groups noticed any increased effectiveness?
4. Has the self-esteem of any of your students been affected in a positive way by their development and practice of collaboration skills?

VII. SUGGESTED READING

Avery, Christopher M. *Teamwork is An Individual Skill: Getting Your Work Done When Sharing Responsibility*. San Francisco, CA: Berrett-Koehler Publishers, Inc., 2001.

Goetsch, David L. *Effective Teamwork: Ten Steps for Technical Professions*. Upper Saddle River, New Jersey: Pearson, Prentice Hall, 2004.

Markova, Dawna., Angie McArthur. *Collaborative Intelligence: Thinking with People Who Think Differently*. New York, NY: Spiegel and Grau, 2015.

Morris, Peter. *Dysfunctional Workplace: From Chaos to Collaboration—a Guide to Keeping Sane on the Job*. Avon, MA: F and W Publications, Co., 2008.

Pearl, Amy A., Stephanie D. Phibbs and Diane Roesch. *The Collaboration Breakthrough*. Charleston, SC: Advantage, 2015.

Tharp, Twyla. *The Collaborative Habit: Life Lessons for Working Together*. New York, NY: Simon and Schuster, 2009.

VIII. REFERENCES

1. Wynton Marsalis and Geoffrey Ward, *Moving to Higher Ground: How Jazz Can Change Your Life* (New York, NY: Random House, 2008), 5.
2. Arthur R. Pell, *The Complete Idiot's Guide to Team Building* (Indianapolis, IN: Alpha Books, 1999), 5.
3. Keith Sawyer, *Group Genius: The Creative Power of Collaboration* (New York, NY: Basic Books, 2007), 8.
4. Arthur R. Pell, Ibid, 5.
5. University of Strathclyde, Glasgow. *Teamwork and Collaboration Skills*. http://www.strath.ac.uk/professionalservices/careers/skills/peopleskills/teamworkcollaborationskills/ (accessed 7-10-14)
6. 18. Ibid.

IX. NOTES

CHAPTER 7

IMPROVISATION

"Where does our material come from? The interaction of
sensation, imagination, and memory."
—Ruth Zaporah.[1]

"If improv is all made up spontaneously, then why practice?"
—Edward Nevraumont
and Nicholas Hanson.[2]

I. SKILL IMPORTANCE, CONTEXT, DEFINITION, AND BREAKDOWN

SKILL IMPORTANCE AND CONTEXT

When music students learn the skills needed to improvise, they are learning more than a course requirement; they are gaining a universal skill with significant potential to serve them well throughout all of life. When an unexpected opportunity, situation, or change arises, the ability to make a quick adjustment without a game plan is quite beneficial. This is especially important in today's fluid career environments. At the same time, by studying improvisation, students improve skills invaluable to music and performance. These include understanding music theory on a deeper level to benefit music learning and assimilation speeds, playing what they hear (inner hearing) in the moment to better benefit memorized performance, and generally building overall performance confidence—if something goes awry, extrication becomes easier. Additionally, the wider skill base gained by learning to improvise music helps increase a musician's marketability: musicians who can play from an orchestral score *and* a jazz chart will certainly find more opportunities to play. For these reasons, I include basic improvisation tools in classical piano lessons (transposition, harmonizing melodies, learning multiple-use patterns, and playing by ear). I strongly urge all my students to take a course in jazz improvisation as well.

I teach my students improvisation in their classical piano lessons because it is an invaluable exercise for helping them to stay in the moment and focus. It also helps them acquire the alertness necessary to adjust to all the unexpected changes that can occur during performance. As with all skills in this book, the process of transferring the skill of improvisation from music to non-music applications is promoted as an important option in the lesson—it must not be assumed the process will happen on its own. For most student musicians, gaining improvisation skills will be time well-spent because of the infinite possibility of applications.

WE'RE ALL IMPROVISERS...

When introducing this topic, I always tell my students that they already are good improvisers. That comment usually generates mystified or bemused looks. I continue by saying that they improvise all the time, but unknowingly. More mystified looks. Then I say, having a conversation with a friend is improvisatory—and no matter where conversation goes, following and contributing is usually not a problem. If the topic suddenly moves from the weather to the price of gasoline, neither party would find the change particularly problematic. Transitions from topic to topic are handled with ease and fluency.

BUT NOT IN THIS FIELD...

For many classically-trained musicians, however, improvising on their instrument is not so effortless. How many accomplished classical music students have painfully felt the panic of such a lack in their training when asked to play Happy Birthday on the spot, a patriotic song, or the melody of any popular tune—and couldn't pick out the melody nor harmonize it, much less improvise on it? This lack partially stems from the fact that improvisation is not a requirement in most classical music education programs. This position differs dramatically from past centuries, when improvisation, often in the form of cadenzas or reading (and fleshing out) figured bass, was routinely expected. From the perspective of non-musicians, it just doesn't make sense that a pianist with the skills to play a Beethoven sonata is unable to play a simple piece by ear or improvise a melody. Apart from avoiding the occasional embarrassment, however, there are many other important reasons for learning improvisational skills today, as we'll soon see in this chapter.

SKILL DEFINITION

To make sure we are on the same page, two standard dictionaries give these definitions of improvisation: first, "Create and perform (music, drama, or verse) spontaneously or without preparation,"[3] and second, "…improvised music is not produced without some kind of preconception or point of departure."[4] Improvisation, in other words, is a combination of the ability to function creatively on the fly while tapping into an existing knowledge base.

WHAT IMPROVISATION IS NOT

It is a misconception to think that improvisation is simply making something up on the spot or just grabbing music out of thin air. Jazz saxophonist Charlie Parker said "You've got to learn your instrument. Then, you practice, practice, practice. And then, when you finally get up there on the bandstand, forget all that and just wail."[5] A jazz musician, for example, must already know an existing melody to be able to play it either verbatim or altered. They also must have the skills to play a melody by ear or to invent one. Further, the harmonies used to accompany that melody are derived from an existing musical language of jazz. The "making up" part is actually a process of choosing or expanding from a vast array of pre-existing possibilities and placing them into a sequence that makes sense to the improviser. In essence, nearly every component—such as chord type, mode, sequence, pattern, etc.—of the improvisatory process has already been learned; it's the spontaneity of the decision-making in using pre-learned materials that is left to the last moment, thus creating the improvisatory nature of the performance. Thus, improvisation is not a magical, on-the-spot event—even though it can *sound* that way in the hands of a top performer. The same process can hold true in any discipline: sport, theater, science, etc., as we'll soon see. Improvisation in music, then, is really about working in a language that is already well-known to the performer—just like speaking with a friend. It is not about creating a new language on the spot.

SKILL BREAKDOWN

1. BEING IN THE MOMENT

Improvisation teaches musicians how to remain in the moment, in both musical and non-musical settings. Jazz trumpeter Wynton Marsalis fully concurs, having said "Jazz music is the power of *now*. There is no script. It's conversation."[6] This is crucial for students to understand: "now" is where everything happens. It is the only moment where you can exert an element of control—everything else is a memory or conjecture.

2. ADAPTABILITY

Improvisation can help students become more comfortable working in an environment that is neither static nor predictable. Should sudden changes occur or new demands appear, regardless of the environment, musicians who have developed improvisation skills are likely to be more comfortable reacting to those changes—especially if they have already practiced transferring that skill to other areas of life. In learning to improvise and transfer that skill, students will have become conditioned to better deal with unpredictability and change. For those without such training or experience, however, working in environments with fast-changing conditions can be unsettling and may reduce levels of performance or productivity.

There is another reason learning improvisation is so good for musicians (in both musical and non-musical applications): the skill is necessary to function more effectively in the quickly evolving music marketplace where the application of improvisatory skills must extend *beyond* music performance. Just as a good jazz improviser can capitalize on an unexpected twist in a melody or rhythm during a performance, a musician must also be able to capitalize on an unexpected twist in a career opportunity or life path (in or out of the music field). Swiss music educator Émile Jaques-Dalcroze said "…improvisation's function is to develop rapidity of decision and interpretation, effortless concentration, the immediate conception of plans…"[7] Life presents the unexpected all the time; instead of being confused, flummoxed, despondent, or just unable to react effectively at all, why not develop a skill and a philosophy that enables one to adapt effectively when faced with the unplanned turn of events? In this context, improvisation is about adaptability—and it's something our current music marketplace demands more than ever.

3. THINK LIKE AN ENTREPRENEUR

Improvisation is a skill shared by successful entrepreneurs and jazz musicians alike. Both are able to seize the moment when changing conditions create new opportunities. These new opportunities could ultimately have more potential than the original plan—be on the lookout! That itself is an exciting revelation. Jazz trumpeter Miles Davis said "I'll play it first and tell you what it is later."[8] As I have mentioned, environments containing ever-changing conditions are becoming more the norm in many workforces—music and otherwise. So it is no secret that more and more musicians are finding that they must reinvent themselves in the job market by creating new possibilities and livelihoods for themselves when traditional music careers do not materialize.

Musicians who rigidly adhere to the score may experience an error or an unintended variation during performance as a calamity. But improvisers know how to treat them as opportunities. One person is prepared for change, the other isn't. Becoming comfortable with the principles of improvisation has implications far beyond performance on the instrument itself. In the book, *Beyond the Conservatory Model: Reimagining Classical Music Performance Training in Higher Education*, authors Stepniak and Sirotin quote artist manager Bill Capone on the benefits of students being able to "personally navigate myriad changes in the marketplace" saying "the ability to be flexible and versatile gives them more chance of success."[9] Learning the universal skill of improvisation trains the student to become more versatile and flexible.

4. READINESS TO TRANSFER (TRANSPOSE!) TO NEW MUSIC OPPORTUNITIES OR OTHER FIELDS

Musicians aren't the only ones who must learn to improvise: one of the more desired skills in today's business world is the ability to improvise on one's feet—a necessity in 21st century workplaces. Consultants who offer training to executives in this very skill can readily be found; one of these is Robert Kulhan, who teaches at Duke University's Faqua School of Business in North Carolina and is CEO of Business Improvisations. He says, "Improvisation isn't about comedy. It's about reacting—being focused and present in the moment at a very high level."[10] Another improvisation instructor, Rick Andrews at New York's Magnet Theater, has given hundreds of improv sessions there, including corporate training courses for companies like Google, PepsiCo, MetLife, and McKinsey.[11] There are many recent articles on the importance of improvisation for business executives. For example, in his article "Leadership Agility: Using Improv to Build Critical Skills," Director of Marketing and Business Development of UNC-Chapel Hill Executive Development Kip Kelly asked, "How do you develop agile business leaders in your organization? While knowledge and experience remain critical, it is becoming increasingly important to develop leaders with the ability to deal with ambiguity and change, to lead and foster innovation and creativity, and to make and implement decisions quickly."[12] The widespread phenomenon of this new style of training demonstrates the importance of improvisation in the business world.

For musicians, it too is important to have knowledge and experience. But they, like the business executives mentioned above, must also understand the importance of improvisation and, through it, develop the ability to deal with ambiguity and change in order to lead and foster innovation and creativity. Conductor André Raphel concurs, saying "In addition to being complete musicians, the demand for innovators in the classical field has never been higher."[13]

Clearly, learning improvisation skills and their transference in the context of the music lesson offers another possibility for expanding your students' adaptability and ability to innovate within any profession and throughout life in general.

II. TONIC KEY
Learn to Apply the Skill to Music

The following eight steps are for the classical music teacher who wants to include a basic tutorial on improvisation in lessons. I have found these steps to work well over a broad spectrum of different levels of students who are new to improvisational practices. Teachers who are already well-versed in teaching improvisation and who have already included that training in their students' lessons may wish to skip ahead to the "pivot chord" section in this chapter.

1. IDENTIFY COMFORT LEVELS AND ZONES

Ask your student to play random notes and/or chords on their instrument. How does that make them feel? Note their reactions; the more discomfort they exhibit, the more nudging they may need to release their reticence towards improvisation. For the more introverted and/or inhibited students, play along with them, saying, "Let's both look and sound silly together."

2. PROGRAMMATIC CONNECTIONS

Challenge students to mimic certain sounds in nature, such as water, wind, lightning, horses' hooves, etc., on their instrument. Emphasize the importance of working with the skills they already have, rather than on what they cannot do, since the latter invariably defeats the purpose of the exercise. Even a rudimentary technique on an instrument allows for exploration and success.

3. SAY "YES" TO THE UNEXPECTED—EXPERIENCE "ANYTHING GOES"

Ask students to play a random series of notes—perhaps just whole tones, or the first five notes of a particular key, while you repeat a sequence of I, IV, and V chords on the piano. You can do this in any number of styles, such as boogie-woogie. This exercise helps free students to both explore and recognize that playing uncharted notes can actually be quite liberating—and can actually sound good, too. This may also help them begin to come to terms with their restrictive habit of thinking that there is only one way of doing something. For many students, classical music study tends to engender such a habit because the score seems to dictate so much specificity.

4. LISTEN AND DISCOVER

Listening is a major component of improvisation; if a student is not listening well, how can they respond? To help get a sense of how your student listens, have them describe in great detail some sounds (that you create for them). For example: rip a piece of paper slowly, then again quickly—did it have a duration and pitch? Drop a pen—how many times did it bounce, what sound accompanied each bounce, and how were they different? Sing a long tone—change it in as many ways as you can (using dynamics, timbre, and vibrato) and ask the student to recount, in order, all the changes. Once a student becomes adept at gathering aural information, they will have more material to inform their response. For example, while a student is playing random notes in step three, found above, they may become more aware of a particularly satisfying combination of notes and rhythms upon which they could build an entire composition—something which may not have occurred to them earlier.

5. ADDING POSSIBILITIES

For piano students using this exercise, introduce first the use of primary chords to accompany a simple melody. Hopefully, this step will help generate more enthusiasm about the improvisatory process and its potential, inspiring them to go further. Other instrumentalists could write out a few primary chords to a melody for their teacher to play on the piano while they play the melody on their instrument.

6. VARIATIONS ON A THEME

As your students become more comfortable with basic improvisation, they can start practicing simple theme and variation steps, beginning first with the melody. The premise of theme and variation is that one works from an existing template (such as the melody) and then varies it. For example, if an existing melody ascends and descends in quarter notes and in intervals of thirds, it could be varied by adding passing tones in eighth notes, using appoggiaturas, or changing the modality, tempo, or rhythm. The possibilities are almost endless.

7. INCREASE COMPLEXITY

Ask your piano student to harmonize, using not only the I, IV, and V chords, but including the ii, iii, vi, and vii° chords as well. Later, they may add secondary dominants. Have them experiment using the same melody with syncopations and varying rhythms. When a student gets to the point where they can use these chords with some fluency, they will experience a newfound freedom— they can now control and create a musical outcome themselves instead of being wholly dependent upon a score. Instrumentalists can work similarly via this basic premise, by using any number of play-along-type recordings, by companies such as Music Minus One.

8. A BIGGER STEP

There are plenty of good available resources for improvisation, such as Jamey Aebersold's *Play-A-Long* series or David Baker's book, *Jazz Improvisation: A Comprehensive Method for All Musicians*. For the younger instrumentalist, Mike Steinel's *Essential Elements for Jazz Ensemble* is a good resource. Piano series, such as the Robert Pace, Faber & Faber, and Helen Malais methods, offer many improvisation opportunities for the younger student and make it easy for a teacher to include teaching this skill early in their students' lessons.

III. PIVOT CHORD
Prepare to Transpose the Skill to a Non-Music Application

Once your student becomes comfortable with the basic elements of music improvisation, it's time to introduce the importance of transferring this skill to non-music areas. The steps for music improvisation are the same as the steps for non-music improvisation (much like the pitches in a pivot chord are common to two key areas). The teacher does not need expertise in the non-music area. Remind the student about the ubiquitous role improvisation already plays in life, such as in conversation or in deciphering a new route when a road becomes blocked. This awareness may help them begin to view improvisation as a universal and necessary skill for use throughout life and as something that will help them adapt more readily to the unexpected twists and turns that can occur.

I always help students make the connection to how universal skills used in music can also benefit the bigger picture in life and work. My experience has shown me that students usually do not make this step on their own. Below are some steps I use to transfer improvisation from music to non-music areas.

IV. TRANSPOSITION
Actively Transpose the Skill to a Non-Music Application

Here, I will use some of the same basic steps found in the music application section above and direct them to non-music applications.

1. IDENTIFY COMFORT LEVELS

If your student had difficulty getting beyond the unpredictable nature of improvisation in music, they may also feel uncomfortable when this skill becomes necessary in a non-music application. They needn't feel alone: there's a reason why so many people dislike having to deal with unpredictable situations in work and business—because it makes them feel unprepared and, hence, vulnerable. Which is precisely why it is so important to become more comfortable with the skill of improvisation because of the increasingly fluid and fast-changing nature of many workplaces (including the music marketplace).

Exercise: The goal here is to help students who are uncomfortable with the unexpected to consider a different or less resistant reaction when faced with an unexpected turn of events. Remind your students to recall the same initial steps they used while improvising in music and what they did to push through their initial resistance, such as starting simply and with few expectations. Also remind them to take note of their feelings, but to do so without judgement. For example, if their self-talk veers to "I really hate trying this and I'll never do it again" it would be constructive to instead redirect the self-talk to something like "I am uncomfortable with this, but my earlier music improvisation experiences have shown me that I become more comfortable if I stick with it and remain less judgmental in the process."

2. PRACTICE IMPROVISATION

Impress upon your student that the best thing they can do is to include a little improvisation each day (no matter what the situation) in order to become more comfortable and adapt to the process.

Exercise: Ask the student to do an exercise outside their lesson, such as striking up a conversation with someone they usually don't talk with, perhaps a fellow student they don't know or a cashier. As mentioned, talking with someone is real improvisation—you never know where the conversation will go and what will be asked next. After doing so, how did it make the student feel? Do they begin to feel more comfortable over time while being in an unpredictable situation? As with anything, practice makes better.

3. SAY "YES" TO THE UNEXPECTED

Remind students that the unexpected will always be a part of their lives—*how* one reacts to a new turn of events is key. Ask them to consider, this time, going along with an unexpected turn of events, seeing where it leads, and making the most of it instead of fighting or resisting the change. Can they think of a past example where this may have happened?

Exercise: Ask your student about a time when a change of events negatively impacted them in the past. Was their day ruined? Were they unable to adjust comfortably to a new plan for the day? If so, suggest that next time they try saying "yes" to the new situation, try to minimize their objections, and see where it leads. This approach can be applied in a work or social situation. Here, the most important thing to keep in mind is to try being more accepting of the new situation and less resistant to it—perhaps even curious. Doing so can start another chain of events which might present all sorts of possibilities. The opposite response leaves zero possibility for anything to progress further.

4. LISTEN AND DISCOVER

Good improvisers are alert to input and their surroundings. The more detail they can gather, the more material they have to work with—creating a deeper well to draw from if improvising becomes necessary. To help increase your student's "gathering" ability, ask them to spend five or ten minutes outside without an electronic device while they walk in nature or down a street. Ask them to take in all the sights and sounds around them, then try to recall as many of them as they can in a minute. Have them try this each day for a week. Ask them at their next lesson if they became more aware of their surroundings and adept at recall. Remind them that awareness of other people and environment helps provide fresh information from which to create new responses and trajectories—this is the key to good improvisation.

Exercise: In this transference part of the lesson, encourage your student to assume a very *aware* state when they are in a situation that requires them to act on the fly with no preparation. Remind them that acquiring information in such a situation allows for better decision making. Perhaps your piano student has been asked to "fill in" during a band rehearsal on a marimba part using a digital keyboard. Would they say no or would they say "yes" to the unexpected—and perhaps open up a whole new realm of opportunities, including using synthesizers on gigs? Once they said yes, they realized they could learn a great deal about how to play their percussion part on the synthesizer just by being very aware of the other "real" percussion players around them.

5. VARIATIONS ON A THEME

In this exercise, your student is required to function spontaneously, with no idea where the situation may lead, but they are verbally riffing off a stated theme.

Exercise: Suggest to your student that they might practice improvisational play-acting with a friend. Select a topic, and then both just make up lines and scenarios that respond to the other— each creating variations based upon a central theme. For example: Person 1: "I heard that your dog could talk!" Person 2: "Whoa! You know that?" Person 1: "Yeah, your sister told me." Person 2: "OK, so the dog can talk, but keep it to yourself!" Continue in the same fashion.

EXTENDED TRANSFERENCE SCENARIO: IMPROVISATION SKILL APPLIED IN A NON-MUSIC FIELD

A music teacher asks her oboe student, Katelyn, to think about where improvisational skills could benefit her outside of music—in her part-time job, or in sports, or in another class, perhaps? Katelyn answers that she has a job at a local retail store where her boss asks people to fill in without notice for other employees who don't show up for work. Sometimes the tasks are quite new and different and would be significantly out of her comfort range if she were asked to do them. The teacher asks Katelyn, whose regular job is to work at the register, what different tasks might be asked of her. She said she might be asked to work on the floor at some point—to greet customers and help them with merchandise choices. She went on to say that if asked, she would agree to try, but she probably would be uncomfortable and very concerned that she wouldn't do well.

The teacher hears Katelyn's reply, but does not need to know anything about the retail business in order to help her transfer her musical improvisation skills to the new task. Here are a few examples of how the teacher could ask questions to help Katelyn figure out how to make the skill transfer for herself:

1. START WITH WHAT YOU KNOW—AND MENTALLY SAY "YES"

Just as you would draw from previously learned ingredients of melodies and harmonies in order to improvise in music, improvising in another area can work in a similar way. Ask your student, "What do you *already know* about greeting a customer?" Although Katelyn was not trained for that particular position on the floor, she realizes she already has the ingredients to accomplish the job: greeting the customer with a warm smile was something she already did at the register, but now, she would add the official store greeting, which was something she had not used, but come to think about it, had heard hundreds of times. What do you *already know* about your surroundings (the layout of the store)? Even though Katelyn has not been specifically trained to know where all the merchandise is, having worked in the store for some time, she knows the men's and women's sections are on different sides of the store and generally knows where different types and styles of clothes can be found. Again, she has enough information to function at a reasonable level—even though she did not think so at first. She will also try to gather as much relevant information as she can as the day progresses.

2. KNOW THAT AN IMPROVISED PERFORMANCE IS NOT ALWAYS GOING TO BE PERFECT

Remember, it's not about perfect. A jazz musician does not expect to nail every note or musical idea in an improvised performance, so why should someone expect to do so in a different situation that requires improvisation? In other words, discuss the idea of becoming more comfortable with making a few errors; plus, they're often negligible in the big picture. The teacher asks Katelyn: "Is it possible that you might make a few mistakes when looking for customers' requests? Is that okay? How would you be able to quickly adjust, somehow find the right answer, and make the experience helpful and expedient for the customer?"

3. IMPROVISATION IS LIKE A GAME

For music improvisers, much of the fun is to see where a new path may lead. In sports, especially team sports, one never knows exactly what is going to happen next—and, as in music, improvisation is also one of the primary and pleasing elements of the game! As we know from experience, well-laid game plans can crumble in an instant. For example, when a quarterback can't find his intended target, he has to run the ball instead, or quickly search for a new receiver—totally improvised, but not wholly unplanned for. The teacher asks Katelyn to consider adopting this sort of attitude when a work situation calls for improvisatory skills. Instead of being knocked off balance after having to diverge from an established plan, can she react to the change with a spirit of play? That "sense of a game" is precisely what Katelyn learns to adopt when, at the last moment, she actually is asked to fill-in for a store position for which she has no experience.

4. ENJOYING THE SPONTANEITY OF THE MOMENT

One of the benefits of working in a situation where improvisation is required is the pleasure derived from being creative and spontaneous—it can be both challenging and exciting, and quite the opposite of doing cookie-cutter work! The teacher asks Katelyn at her next lesson to tell what happened when she had to improvise in her new position at her job. Katelyn says she initially became a little flustered when she was not sure of something in her new role. But soon she found a better way to manage; if asked a question to which she did not know the answer she simply acknowledged that fact and then quickly found someone who did. In another instance, Katelyn had occasion to use her prior "walking down the street and taking it all in" exercise. She made a point of figuring out the entire stockroom layout by her third trip, thus reducing her search times considerably for the remainder of the day.

Talking with her music teacher in advance about improvising in the sales job reduced her anxiety. The walking exercise done outside of the lesson gave her the presence of mind to analyze the stockroom's layout, while at the same time looking for a particular item. Katelyn had also recast the tasks in her mind as a "game" requiring improvisational skill, born out of necessity and devised in the moment, instead of viewing it as an uncomfortable day on the job.

V. RECAP
Revisit the Skill in Music

Remind your students that improvisation is not about blindly making something up, such as reaching into a spice cabinet and dumping the contents of whatever is first grasped into the pot. Rather, it is about reacting to new conditions and successfully implementing or combining *known* information in new and previously unplanned ways. Improvisation is not only a musical skill, but also a life skill that should be a part of all musicians' toolkits.

Circling back: how might have Katelyn's experience improvising as a sales clerk added a deeper understanding and better use of that skill in music? Could it have increased her ability to experiment with a wider range of interpretational possibilities when preparing for a performance? Can Katelyn re-apply the improvisational steps she practiced in her retail job to writing and performing a cadenza with more confidence? Might she use less negative self-talk when something doesn't go according to her expectations?

VI. QUESTIONS FOR REFLECTION

1. Where do your students think improvisational skills could benefit them outside music—in a job, in sports, in another class, or to fix something that is broken? Where else do they sometimes need to think extemporaneously? Have they seen someone else exercise this skill especially successfully? Did they learn something from it?
2. Can past experiences or knowledge help them improvise a solution in a predicament?

3. While improvising, can they identify what they already know about the subject? Can they use that as a starting point? Can they adopt a robust yes-I-can attitude?

4. Have they relinquished the stance that every outcome needs to be "perfect?" Do they feel more comfortable when making mistakes?

5. If your students are knocked off balance or if they become uncomfortable improvising, can they think about maintaining a "game-like spirit" to help the experience remain on track? Can they make the improvisational process fun regardless of the outcome?

6. Ask your students to review past improvisation experiences: What happened when they tried to improvise? How did they manage (or at least try to) when something unexpected happened? Were they able to recast it in a positive way in their mind and move on?

VII. SUGGESTED READING

Aebersold, Jamey. *How To Play Jazz and Improvise*, vol. 1. New Albany, IN: Jamey Aebersold Jazz, Inc., 1992.

Baker, David. *Jazz Improvisation: A Comprehensive Method for All Musicians*. Van Nuys, CA: Alfred Publishing, Co., 1988.

Bergren, Mark; Cox, Molly; and Detmar, Jim. *Improvise This: How to Think on Your Feet So You Don't Fall on Your Face*. New York, NY: Hyperion, 2002.

Fey, Tina. *Bossypants*. New York, NY: Little Brown and Co., 2011.

Findlay, Elsa. *Rhythm and Movement: Applications of Dalcroze Eurhythmics*. Miami, FL: Summy-Birchard, 1995.

Goodkin, Doug. *Play, Sing and Dance: An Introduction to Orff-Schulwerke*. London, UK: Schott, 2002.

Gordon, Edwin E. *Primary Measures of Audiation*. Chicago, IL: GIA Publications, Inc., 1979.

Leonard, Kelly and Yorton, Tom. *Yes, And: How Improvisation Reverses "No, But" Thinking and Improves Creativity and Collaboration*. New York, NY: Harper Collins, 2015.

Steinel, Mike. *For Piano, Essential Elements for Jazz Ensemble: A Comprehensive Method for Jazz Style and Improvisation*. Milwaukee, WI: Hal Leonard, 2000.

VIII. REFERENCES

1. Ruth Zaporah, *Action Theater: The Improvisation of Presence* (Berkeley, CA: North Atlantic Books, 1995), 17.

2. Edward J. Nevaurumont and Nicholas P. Hanson, *The Ultimate Improv Book: A Complete Guide to Comedy Improvisation* (Englewood, CO: Meriwether Publishing, 2001), 3.

3. Oxford English Dictionary Online, "improvise." www.oxforddictionaries. com/us/definition/american_english/improvise (accessed 1-15-18)

4. Don Michael Randel, *The New Harvard Dictionary of Music* (Cambridge, MA: The Belknap Press of Harvard University Press, 1986), 392.

5. William Safire and Leonard Safir, *Words of Wisdom* (New York, New York: Simon & Schuster 1990), 79.

6. Wynton Marsalis and Geoffrey Ward, *Moving to Higher Ground: How Jazz Can Change Your Life* (New York, NY: Random House, 2008), 8.

7. Émile Jaques Dalcroze, trans. F. Rothwell, "Rhythmics and Pianoforte Improvisation," *Music and Letters* 13 (1932) 371.

8. John Szwed, *So What: The Life of Miles Davis* (New York, NY: Random House, 2012).

9. Michael Stepniak and Peter Sirotin, *Beyond the Conservatory Model: Reimagining Classical Music Performance Training in Higher Music Education* (New York, NY: Routledge, 2020), 35.

10. Mark Tutton, "Why Using Improvisation to Teach Business Skills is No Joke," CNN Online (2-18-2010), www.cnn.com/2010/BUSINESS/02/18/improvisation.business.skills/ (accessed 11-17-16).

11. Jesse Scinto, "Why Improv Training is Great Business Training," *Forbes* Online (6-27-2014). www.forbes.com/sites/forbesleadershipforum/2014/06/27/why-improv-training-is-great-business-training/ (accessed 4-18-17).

12. Kip Kelly, "Leadership Agility: Using Improv to Build Critical Skills," UNC Kenan-Flager Business School online publication (2012), 2 http://execdev.kenan-flagler.unc.edu/blog/leadership-agility-using-improv-to-build-critical-skills (accessed 2-14-18)

13. Michael Stepniak and Peter Sirotin, *Beyond the Conservatory Model: Reimagining Classical Music Performance Training in Higher Music Education* (New York, NY: Routledge, 2020), 35.

IX. NOTES

CHAPTER 8

CREATIVITY

"Creativity is our birthright. It is an integral part of being a human, as basic as walking, talking, and thinking."
—John Daido Loori.[1]

"What a good artist understands is that nothing comes from nowhere. All creative work builds on what came before. Nothing is completely original."
—Austin Kleon.[2]

"Don't wait for the proverbial apple to fall on your head. Go out into the world and proactively seek experiences that will spark creative thinking."
—Tom and David Kelly.[3]

"There is nothing new under the sun."
—Ecclesiastes 1:9.[4]

I. SKILL IMPORTANCE, CONTEXT, DEFINITION, AND BREAKDOWN

SKILL IMPORTANCE

In my estimation, creativity is *the* most essential skill a musician can have. From creativity comes expressiveness, communication, the ability to move audiences, originality, authenticity, and more. It is the performer's creative voice that transports music to a place where it becomes engaging, interesting, expressive, and captivating. I think we all would agree that creativity is at the core of a great musician. Not surprisingly, many of the other universal skills play a significant role in informing the creative process. How would creativity thrive without focus, communication, problem-solving, etc.? Creativity, in return, also informs and benefits every skill mentioned in this book. This idea of symbiosis is a recurring principle in each of these chapters. It is the act of transferring a universal skill from a music application to a non-music application *and back again* to create a mutually beneficial relationship—each application helps to further benefit and inform the other. I have called this process the cross-training circle.

Up to now, however, I have used this cross-training circle idea only as it applies to a *single* universal skill, where diverse applications (music and non-music uses) of a single skill reinforce and improve its use overall. However, the cross-training circle can *also* exist between the universal skills themselves. For example, problem-solving can benefit creativity and vice-versa or focus can benefit critical thinking and vice-versa, etc. As your students become well-versed in applying these universal skills to their music and transferring them to all of life, it is important, ultimately, for them to also see a still bigger picture: where *all* universal skills are intrinsically linked and continue to inform and benefit one another. I am well aware that this "bigger view" takes time and maturity to develop, but it is exponentially worth the effort to nurture this perspective because of the insights and advantages it will produce over a lifetime.

This perspective is especially relevant these days because musicians are called upon to apply their creativity not only to performing the repertoire itself but also to every aspect of their careers, including programming, publicity, branding, arts advocacy, audience-building, and all the myriad entrepreneurial steps involved in each. Because of the breadth of those demands, musicians' creative skills will be continually challenged and expanded!

With those demands in mind, most of us would agree that creativity is a pretty important skill to develop and nurture in our students. But how do we teach this important and elusive element in our lessons? Hasn't creativity often been described as something that you either have or don't? If a student comes by creativity naturally and easily, great, we're off the hook. But what if some students don't come to it as easily? What then? Is it possible to explain what creativity is and, more importantly, is it possible to teach it? I have found a way to explain and teach creativity through a series of simple steps that work well for my piano students. Before I enumerate the steps I have found to be helpful, a few more words on creativity itself and how some musicians have used it to their advantage.

SKILL CONTEXT

HIGHLY CREATIVE MUSICIANS AND ENSEMBLES

Some musicians, as part of their creative processes, have added new twists or elements to traditional formats. Solo drummer Ian Chang chooses to mix analog and electronic means to produce a dizzying array of percussion sounds. The Canadian Brass adds popular music, humor, and dialogue to their concerts. The Kronos Quartet, in addition to only playing recently-composed music, chooses to perform in edgy, hip clothes. The Phillip Glass Ensemble takes the idea of repetition and patterns, so common in music and nature, to a whole new level in music. The Anderson and Rowe Duo capitalizes upon intersections between two-piano music and theatre and film. Adding a twist to an existing format, of course, gives no guarantee of success, but it sure can help your chances. It is not surprising then, when an imaginative twist combines with high levels of proficiency and determination, that a musician or ensemble may have more success in attracting audiences than those who try a traditional, well-worn route.

SKILL DEFINITION

Although the following two definitions and perspectives on creativity provide a good start, they also illustrate the difficulty of providing a sense of just what creativity is. The *New Oxford American Dictionary* defines creativity as "the use of the imagination or original ideas, esp. in the production of an artistic work."[5]

Gregory Feist in the *Cambridge Handbook of Creativity* provides a wider perspective of creativity: "As a long-time creativity researcher, I often hear, especially from artists, that creativity is inherently unknowable, mysterious, and immeasurable. Hence, the argument continues, researchers can't agree even on what creativity means. It may be true that creativity is difficult to measure and to quantify, but it's not impossible and it is false to say no consensual definition has emerged. In fact, creativity researchers have for the last 60 years been nearly unanimous in their definition of the concept (e.g., Amabile, 1996; Feist, 2006; Guilford, 1950; Kaufman and Baer, 2004; MacKinnon, 1970; Runco, 2004; Simonton, 2008; Sternberg, 1988): Creative thought or behavior must be both novel/original and useful/adaptive."[6]

The first quote is merely a bare-bones explanation that reveals very little about creativity other than it must be imaginative and original. The second quote, in essence, states that creativity should not only be original but have a useful or adaptive purpose. What's interesting about that last quote is that the very people who epitomize creativity in their work (artists) are often the same ones who say the creative process is "unknowable," and "mysterious." I have also heard many musicians, visual artists, and poets echo that belief. These are people who do creative things day in and day out (and who mentor or teach young artists), yet say they can't define what creativity is.

These examples might explain, in part, why students working in the creative arts are so often left to discover the nature of the creative process on their own. This is no bad thing in itself…we certainly have no shortage of artists doing wonderfully creative things. But what if there were an easily understood process—taking us beyond these basic definitions—to help more students further develop and increase their levels of creativity? This chapter, then, explores the notion that creativity—the novel/original and useful/adaptive thoughts and behaviors—can be stimulated, and, yes, learned and developed as a process.

Indeed, the great cellist, Yo-Yo Ma, consciously stimulated his own musical creativity and development through his long-term Silk Road Project. There, he adopted an ecological phrase, called the edge effect—something he describes as "when two ecosystems meet and you have the least density but the greatest variety."[7] He has used that phrase as a metaphor to depict the cross-culturalism deeply imbedded in that project's DNA and all the creative possibilities that emanate from those cultural interactions.

Here's yet another look at an aspect of the creative process which may help expand the notion of what it is. In Frans Johansson's book, *The Medici Effect: What Elephants and Epidemics Can Teach Us About Innovation,* he suggests that creativity has a great chance of occurring at the intersections found between disparate fields of study and ideas.[8] An intersection is a place where two different fields share a similar idea or concept. For example, one intersection shared between sports and piano playing is efficiency of movement. Without understanding and managing physical motion (a big part of efficiency), you can't function well in music or sports.

SKILL BREAKDOWN

CREATIVITY IS NOT MAGIC—IT'S THE USE OF VARIATION

Creativity almost always manifests itself through the process of variation. I tell my students that creativity is not some magical act where a great idea appears out of nowhere or is bestowed through divine inspiration to a select few. I also dispel any notion they may have that creativity is either something you have or you don't. Instead, I tell them that creativity is something that comes about through a process of creating new combinations of *existing* elements and information. In other words, creativity is actually theme and variations well-exercised.

This holds true with almost any invention. One of the most innovative and imaginative inventions, the smartphone, is a good example. The smartphone's "newness" came from *combining* long-existing technologies such as the digital camera, phone, computer, GPS, etc., into a small, portable device. Let's remember, none of those technologies were new in themselves—it was the act of combining them all into one small device, with all their limitless interactions and applications that made the smartphone so new and inventive. And there, in this most extraordinary and world-changing device, you see the simple use of variation clearly at work. Over time, engineers continued varying the smartphone by adding this, this, and oh, this too. Rarely is something so wholly new that it just didn't exist on any level before. Instead, invention almost always has a significant connection to something that already exists. In essence, creativity emanates from a series of essential building blocks, which I will illustrate soon.

If there were one step in this chapter I would rank above all others to help define and engage the creative process, it is theme and variation (found in step 10 in the following section).

II. TONIC KEY
Learn to Apply the Skill to Music

TEN STEPS TO PROMOTE CREATIVITY

I. YOU CAN'T CREATE VERY WELL WITHOUT HAVING SOME SKILL LEVEL

In other words, you need to know something about the area or discipline in which you wish to be creative: be it a musical instrument, a paintbrush, words, etc. The exciting news is: the higher the skill level, the greater the possibilities for creativity. So, as you get better, your creative possibilities increase as well! As a musician, you must have some level of skill at an instrument in order to engage creativity. Otherwise, you are left merely struggling to make the instrument produce the simplest of sounds. This does not mean, however, that the early-level student cannot start exercising some creativity in their playing. As soon as they start making dynamic modulations or use rubato, for example, a level of creativity is being exercised. In general, though, the beginning student may find their creative efforts limited for a while until they build up some proficiency with their instrument.

Exercise: This point can be made so easily! Ask your student to think about picking up an instrument that they have never practiced before and imagine trying to be creative with it. Could they vary existing elements such as tempo, dynamics, articulations, or mood? They will immediately understand your point and hopefully jettison any notion they may previously have had that they can contribute creatively to a process in which they have little or no experience.

Summation: Students need to understand the connection and importance of *skill* to the creative process. Without skill, they will find it difficult to manipulate their materials and create at any meaningful level (notes, words, brush strokes, etc.).

2. BREADTH OF KNOWLEDGE

In addition to the need for some skill on an instrument, students need exposure to a wide range of performances, musical styles, and composers to help elevate their awareness of what's already out there and what can be done. It's tough to create in a vacuum. Imagine a pianist having gained great facility on exercises alone, but without having played or heard a single note of actual music. Where would that pianist's musical inventiveness or musicality come from? She wouldn't have much. And that's because inventiveness in music (or any other field) is enabled first from having prior exposure to and a diversity of knowledge within the discipline itself. For musicians, having an awareness of what is currently being done in their field (such as the development of extended instrumental techniques, the past and evolving treatment of performance practice, or the inclusion of new technology) is important to developing their musical acumen.

For a visual example of this, the same necessity for past and present awareness would hold true if you were on a design team at GM, working on the next generation Corvette. To contribute well, you would first have to be familiar with all prior and current Corvette designs—in addition to the general design philosophy of the team—in order to help create a sports car shape that is both new and yet one that still maintains roots to the original 1953 design. In the same way, a musician needs a certain awareness of past and current performance practices in order to be both fresh and relevant in their musical creativity.

Exercise: For your intermediate and advanced level player, ask them to listen to a piece they are currently learning as performed by three or four different artists and carefully take note of the differences or variations between them. Perhaps one artist brought out a wider range of dynamics, another may have played with a great deal more rubato, still another may have played with sparse pedal, etc. After your student has heard and reflected on each interpretation, ask them to insert one distinctive element from each of those performances into their *own* performance. To help them remember, have students write into the score a description of each of the elements they wish to use and where. After the student has practiced those additions into a piece, listen to them in the next lesson. Did you hear the changes and did they improve anything from a creative perspective? Could your student clearly articulate what he had added, both in word and in the performance? Discuss how the piece has changed. Regardless of the results of that exercise, did he feel that he expanded his awareness of the creative possibilities at his disposal?

In this example, the student is, admittedly, using ideas from other artists and incorporating them into his own playing. Soon, however, your students will become expert "borrowers" in the sense that what they hear others do at their instruments now becomes "grist" for their own mill and not mere duplication. This process is certainly not a bad thing; creative artists have "borrowed" from one another since the beginning of time. I have found that my students' imaginations have been ignited after doing this exercise. Remember, this is a start, not the end game. In time, your students will be expressing more and more of their own creative amalgam.

Summation: Help your students understand that their creativity can be greatly stimulated by listening carefully to the performances of top musicians and emulating what they hear. In doing so, they are significantly expanding their awareness of *what is possible*. This is not meant merely as a copy exercise, but one which will grow their awareness of the possibilities. In other words, the more they know about something, the more they can bring to their own creative processes.

3. DEFINE THE PARAMETERS

Without parameters it is very difficult to be creative. Parameters do not impede the creative process; indeed, they most often stimulate it. For example, if someone commissioned a composer to write a piece of music but gave no instructions, it would be difficult for that composer to know just where to start. Without the aid of some guidelines, the composer would have to impose some themselves— the composition, after all, has to take *some* form and have *some* type of instrumentation. However, had the composer been given specific directives, such as: write a chamber music piece that is ten minutes long utilizing eight string instruments in a single movement that is programmatic in nature, the composer's creative energies now have a very specific path to follow.

For a performing musician, many parameters have already been established in the score through a multitude of directives. However, for an interpretation to take shape, a musician still has many other parameters to establish: What character should be infused in the piece; how fast is the Presto going to be; if a dynamic marking is forte, doesn't its loudness level have to be relative to a softer dynamic; and how much artistic liberty is going to be taken? All those parameters (and more) have to be determined and firmly in the mind of the performer before a credible performance can occur—yet, they do not limit an interpretation at all and can actually increase the creative possibilities. This often comes as a surprise to my students.

Exercise: Ask your student to begin establishing parameters with each element or aspect of the music they will be using. Parameters, in this case, means establishing the exact usage (and limits) of elements such as tempo, rubato, dynamic levels, articulations, phrase shapes, and so on. Ask students to succinctly define the scope of each of these parameters into the score by writing out directives as clearly and succinctly as possible, exactly where they wish to apply them. For example, they might write: "play as dry and articulated as possible" or, in another place, "with as much dynamic contrast as possible." Next, students would begin practicing their directives as accurately as possible. Then, ask them to mull the results. Did all the specific parameter limitations contribute to, or detract from, a clear and imaginative interpretation? I think your students will clearly see how parameters increase creative possibilities and greatly contribute to clarity of intent.

Summation: Encourage students to think of parameters as creative stimulators, not inhibitors. By thinking of parameters in this way, students may be amazed at how little restriction there actually is to their imagination.

4. EXPERIMENTATION

Promote the idea with students that they can learn to become comfortable with experimentation. Venturing into the unknown can certainly cause trepidation and unease. Yet, without the spirit of exploration, many creative opportunities may be lost. For example, it is common for a student to be confused as to what direction to take in a certain spot in a piece they are practicing. Instead of waiting until the next lesson for suggestions, students must be encouraged to experiment: they might try a different character with the piece, a few different ways of executing a trill, or a few different tempos and variations of articulation. Making clear to your students that experimentation is part of the creative process gives them the OK to venture beyond the self-imposed restrictions of doing what they think the teacher wants them to do. In all instances of experimentation, the student must be ever-observant to what unfolds and open to recognizing whatever interpretive gem they might have just discovered.

Exercise: Many possibilities can be created to help students practice experimenting; I encourage teachers to design their own exercises for their students, if they haven't already. Here are some I suggest for my students:

1. Play the passage in question doubly slow.
2. Play it twice as loud and with excessive feeling.
3. Play it with absolutely no emotion or tempo change whatsoever.
4. Play it faster than you can manage, but keep going... approximate if necessary.
5. Improvise a waltz entirely made up of "wrong" notes and play it with exaggerated emotion and abandonment (just as they did when practicing improvisation—it's experimentation, too).

If your student just doesn't know where to start in the waltz exercise, ask them to make up notes in an "oom-pah-pah" manner…literally anything their hand falls onto. Suggest they play clumps of notes in the LH and add any kind of single note melody in the RH. Make sure your student does not stop for at least thirty seconds in order to acclimatize to the discomfort and oddness of hearing "wrong" notes. Push them to combat the natural resistance they will invariably feel at first (they will want to stop well short of that already short time period). This exercise can help lead students to apply more experimentation in their playing, a most necessary component in the creative process.

These exercises demonstrate the importance of taking creative steps to the extreme. By doing so, your students dramatically increase their sense of what works and what doesn't—boundaries (parameters) come into view! In this way, they begin establishing their own unique sensibilities. This is a major step forward in the development of establishing a singular, creative voice.

Summation: Experimentation is a significant part of the creative process (experts engage this important component of the creative process liberally) and it can be practiced at any level and with any musical element or combination of elements. Also consider using improvisation (see Chapter Seven) to help your students become more comfortable with experimentation.

5. HARD WORK AND FOCUS

It can be a challenge getting students to the point where they develop a sense of how much diligence and focus are involved in doing creative work. As fun and exciting as it is to think up a great new idea or concept, it still takes hard work to make it manifest. Thinking up something is the easy part; taking it to the finish line is far more difficult. Not surprisingly, taking a piece of music from the first practiced measure to a really good performance (with all the creative requirements needed for such a journey), also takes considerable effort. Help prepare students for this actuality through discussion and inviting small experimental steps at their instrument; this really helps to acclimatize them to the process. Pointing out your students' successes along the way, too, will go a long way to help keep their motivation from flagging.

Exercise: Since mental work is usually the hardest element of practice, developing some skill in audiation (hearing the melody, harmony, and other elements of a piece in the mind's ear) will ensure that students get a taste of the intensity and focus needed to do creative work. Start by asking your students to try audiating (hearing in their inner ear) a short passage in a piece they are already practicing and know well. If possible, have them include expressive elements such as tempo, rubato, articulation, etc. along with melody and harmony. This is a tall order and will take most students some time to manage, even with easier pieces and in short sections. Once they begin to manage the process a bit and can audiate that short passage with some clarity, ask them to imprint an interpretation in their minds, allowing it to become an indelible aural image. This step to the creative process can then be used to guide their practice to eventual performance. For some students, easier steps in this exercise may need to be taken, such as trying to audiate only one expressive element at a time—perhaps just hearing alone the dynamics or rubato they wish to use. Once the student can manage audiating a single element, try adding a second expressive element and then lengthen the sections of the piece being audiated, until the whole piece has been completed. The true effort and time requirements for creative work will soon become apparent to the student. See Chapter Two, Focus, for more detail.

Summation: The above exercise helps students get a sense of the level of work and effort involved in the creative process (so they don't give up prematurely). It can also boost students' levels of satisfaction when they begin to see their efforts come to fruition while working on the creative process of performing a piece or program.

6. DEVELOPING DIVERSE KNOWLEDGE OUTSIDE MUSIC

Many creative breakthroughs and insights can come from ideas generated by looking *outside* one's major area of interest or discipline. I call this process "idea mining." I highly recommend that my students explore new areas both within and outside the field of music (especially outside). Curiosity is critical to the creative process! Suggest to your students that they must be especially alert to identifying shared, common elements between seemingly unrelated things—areas called intersections. For example, what if by listening to a new genre of music, such as Celtic dance music, a piano student was finally able to bring the dance-like quality to a Bach keyboard suite that had always eluded them? What if, by actually watching a glass blower or a flowing mountain stream, a voice student gained a new and effective insight into how to produce and maintain consistent air flow while they sing? As a student, I once through sheer chance gained a deep insight into the importance of fluid motion at the keyboard by seeing a fox "flow" over rough terrain in the woods—there was no up-or-down motion in the body; its lightning-fast legs propelled it effortlessly forward as if on wheels. By playing that ten-second sighting back in my mind, I had an "aha" moment, immediately recognizing the importance of how my hands needed the same ease, suppleness, and fluidity while negotiating "difficult terrain" in my repertoire. That also led me to begin thinking about the importance of physical efficiency (minimal motion) and choreographing gestures in my piano practice. You see, lessons *can* come from decidedly odd places!

In addition to the insight I gained by watching one of nature's most graceful animals move in their habitat, I stumbled upon another insight that originated from my love of skiing and tennis. A little past the mid-twentieth century, trainers in both those and other sports had begun analyzing slow-motion film (and later) video replay to enhance the performance levels of their athletes. It allowed them to better-see and break down complex and inefficient motion to improve the performance levels in their athletes. It also allowed the athletes to clearly view what they were doing wrong—visual clues were often much more indelible and effective than verbal analysis alone. As a graduate student, I read an article in *Popular Mechanics* about the slow-motion camera's use in sports training and immediately saw a connection—that the same application could benefit pianists. That's a real intersection! Soon thereafter, I began applying sports training techniques to piano practice and performance—including biomechanics, interval training, and slow-motion analysis. It became a long-term research and master-class topic. I don't think I would have made that connection had I not had an interest in tennis and skiing or enjoyed reading widely outside my field. I was also very open to considering and exploring at length what I thought were shared intersections. I think that propensity to explore is an important quality to develop in terms of aiding the creative process.

Exercise: Ask your student to tell you about some area outside music in which they have a special interest. Hopefully, you will get a quick response, such as: "Oh, I love being on the debate team!" or, "I really enjoy playing soccer!" Whatever the response, ask your student to see if they can make some connection or find some common ground shared between that interest and their music. Perhaps, in the case of the debate team reply, a student might make the connection between their use of persuasiveness in debating to thinking about how they might be more persuasive conveying a musical idea during performance. They may recognize how the expressive elements in a debate such as pacing, articulation, emotion, dynamics, etc., could be transferred to music to benefit expressiveness, or vice versa.

In the case of the soccer-playing student, perhaps they will have an "aha" moment when they realize how much their physical fitness also benefits their ability to practice their musical instrument; allowing greater energy, endurance, and focus. In this case, the intersection between music performance and soccer is the idea of fitness. Perhaps that realization might trigger the student's interest to delve more deeply into how exercise and even nutrition could benefit a musician physically and mentally for optimal performance on stage. Perhaps that student might also recognize that they developed a good sense of teamwork as a soccer player that could benefit them in their music ensembles. Here, the intersection is teamwork. That is the beauty of exploring intersections—how shared commonality between disciplines can continually inform and benefit one another.

In each example above, the music student could derive something of benefit from a discipline *outside* music which, in turn, could benefit their musical performance. This is the reason for the idea of transference in the lesson—that "circling back" benefit. But this step often needs the help of the teacher to ensure the student makes the connection. (In my experience, this kind of thinking doesn't come naturally to most students.) The process starts with the teacher asking the student to look for common ground (a shared aspect or element) between music and a non-music area and explore how one area might inform the other. The teacher must constantly initiate this concept for the student until it becomes ingrained and natural. I believe all music students can learn something of value from this exercise: it spurs the imagination, breaks down barriers, and stimulates exploration. This is yet another way to encourage and develop an aspect of the creative process in your music students.

Summation: Stepping outside one's specific discipline (comfort zone!) to search for and explore common intersections in other disciplines can lead to uncovering unexpected insights and creative ideas that can benefit the music-making process. Encourage the practice of purposely stepping outside one's usual confines to see what insights might be gained. Attending a popular music concert, for example, might give a classical violinist some creative ideas for her next concert, including how she might employ lighting effects, costumes, interaction with the audience, or perhaps the use of synthesized sounds. Those ideas may have never occurred to her otherwise. It might spark her imagination in never-before explored ways, opening a whole new range of musical possibilities.

7. CLEAR GOALS

Even though it may seem somewhat contradictory to have clear goals for the creative process, it really isn't. Creativity doesn't mean that anything goes or that results just emerge on their own. At the beginning of a project you may not know exactly how the painting or performance may turn out, but you will need specific goals to take you *through* the process. For example, the student needs a pretty clear aural picture of the piece they are about to play if it is to be practiced well. The student might start with defining what type of character is wanted for a particular section, or what sort of articulation is desired in another. They will need to consider the overall dynamic range, how specific passages might be practiced for the eventual high speeds necessary, and what levels of rubato will be applied. If these elements and others aren't being considered during practice and the requisite decisions made, what sort of interpretation is going to emerge? Will it be an interpretation by design or mere happenstance?

Exercise: The next time your student begins a new piece, ask them to be as specific as possible in deciding what expressive choices they will make in the score *before* they start practicing. (This exercise presumes that a student will have some ability to study the score away from their instrument to develop an aural image—audiation—of the sounds they want to create. For more on this, see Chapter Two, Focus.) As mentioned, encourage your students to write clear directives in their scores, articulating exactly what creative choices they want to make and where. All this is done, of course, after the student ponders the score a bit. This exercise will be easier for more advanced musicians, those who have already been able to audiate with some success.

Summation: Having clear goals does not mean that clear end results will be automatically known at the outset. What is important here is that students begin to define a way of thinking; in essence, it's a procedure that will help them start to develop and clarify interpretive goals in a given piece of music.

8. REVERSE ENGINEERING

Reverse engineering is the practice of carefully looking at (dissecting) a successful product to see how it was built and achieved. This is always a good tactic to employ when working creatively. Artists have always scrutinized the work of others in their field. Businesses do too, primarily to keep up with competitor's products and improve their own. This tactic can also be applied to an idea, a thought, a particular way of practicing, or an interpretation in music.

For our music students, there is much to be learned from mining ideas in this way. For example, they can reverse-engineer by carefully studying a score to see exactly what steps a composer took to create variation or thematic development in a piece (Beethoven's music is especially fertile ground for this). Teachers can help in this reverse-engineering process by nudging their students in certain directions or by giving suggestions. Students can watch and listen to top artists perform via YouTube or other sources, to get a sense of how they approach a particular piece musically or from a physical standpoint. If it's for the latter, for example, a student can observe the arm, hand, and finger motions of an accomplished artist for ideas on how to physically manage a section of music that has proven difficult or elusive. There are many insights and perspectives into motion efficiency to be gained from watching top-level artists perform. How, for example, do those professionals make difficult passages look so easy? The (partial) answer: carefully observe their arm, hand, and finger motions. You will see that those artists use just enough motion to achieve their goals and no more...fingers barely clear the keys and most movements are curvilinear (based upon circular gestures). The internet is full of close-up examples in HD for students to view. The reverse engineering possibilities for student musicians today are virtually limitless!

Exercise: After assigning a student their next new piece, have them create an entire interpretation on their own (without any help from you) by using elements that they have reverse-engineered from artists they have heard on YouTube. What elements will they draw upon in the process? Once they have done so, ask them to specifically identify them and what artist used them. Perhaps the student will use elements from only one artist or many. This synthesis of musical ideas, of course, happens to some degree or another with most musicians as they listen to concerts and recordings. What I am showing here is a very conscious approach, designed to help students maximally engage in this practice of reverse-engineering. This exercise is not intended to turn students into "photocopying machines" who merely copy other artists. Rather, it is an exercise to help students gather new ideas to process later in their own way. Finally, have your student perform the "mined" interpretation of the piece they have put together on their own. How does it compare to their past performances?

Summation: Reverse engineering is a very effective way for students to gain insights into the creative process of others and to adapt as they see fit. As I continually mention to my students, most answers are right in front of you—if you only but see them. The reverse engineering process can be enhanced when it is used as a tool with specific goals such as scrutinizing technical or musical elements in the performances of top-flight artists. It must also be mentioned that reverse engineering is ultimately not meant to produce duplications of an existing product or interpretation. It is meant, instead, to give students insights into further creative possibilities without having to reinvent the wheel (creatively speaking). In the best scenario, reverse engineering can reveal valuable insights into a design or piece of music which can then be used by your students to generate something truly innovative and unique of their own. By encouraging your students to become "students of design" (by examining the objects all around them), they become aware of and *really* see the amazingly creative expressions surrounding them each day. Those creative expressions can be found in fashion design, music of all kinds, word, art, architecture, mechanical devices, etc. In every case, the object can deeply and comprehensively inform the observer about its genesis. By looking at the world around them in this way, your students will become keen, expert observers and lifetime students of this non-stop parade of creative examples—all of which can continually develop and inspire their own creative potential.

9. DAYDREAMING

Jonah Lehrer notes that "A daydream is that fountain spurting, spilling strange new thoughts into the stream of consciousness. And these spurts turn out to be surprisingly useful."[9] Consider encouraging your students to let their minds wander sometimes as they look out a window or take a stroll in nature, to help their own "creative fountain" conjure a musical sound or interpretation that could be unique to them, or create an interesting twist in their next recital or presentation in school.

Exercise: To help students get started in this daydreaming process, encourage them to find a conducive environment, such as a quiet place, turn off their electronic devices, and begin by trying to let the mind empty itself of the usual mental clutter and chatter—something not easy to do and which may require repeated attempts and practice (see Chapter Two, Focus, for this step). This quieting-the-mind procedure will help students better position their minds to begin to make free flights of fancy, dream, or just see what materializes. Unlike meditation, however, ridding the mind of all thought is not the goal in daydreaming. Here, the student's goal is to arrive at a place where their mind can freely wander, perch, and examine...perhaps on a particular topic or thing.

PRIMING THE PUMP

Looking at online examples of what other artists have done creatively is great fun and very informative. What if your student is considering making a significant change to the way they are going to approach their next piano recital? They may want to change the traditional format, but where to start with such a notion? By perusing the web, that student just might stumble upon the example of Kathleen Supové and her *Exploding Piano* concerts. Her recital-altering ideas could be transformative. The student might continue exploring by reading the liner notes of one of her CDs[10] to find out how she came to make her dramatic departure from the traditional piano concert. Where did all those ideas for combining narrative, drama, choreography, newly-commissioned works, and acoustic and digital combinations come from? Her concept of what constitutes a piano performance is wildly divergent from most other pianists. There were no previous roadmaps to where she ultimately went. Could Supové have allowed her mind to take free flights of fancy, to dream? Where did her creativity come from? Examination will reveal that every element in her *Exploding Piano* concerts had already long-existed and been widely used in some form or another. For example, light pyrotechnics have been used at rock concerts for decades (Scriabin had ideas for a light show for his work *Mysterium* over a century ago in 1903), choreography has been around for centuries, the digital piano has long been used around the globe at every hotel gig and rock concert since the introduction of the Moog synthesizer in 1964, and visual projections on a screen have also long been used. No, Ms. Supové did not create any of them. It was the creative twist she used by putting them all together in her performances that made her concerts new and riveting. The theme and variation idea is clearly at work here! By making a variant of the piano recital, she rattled the chains of the classical music establishment, forged a new path, and received plenty of attention in the process. Let's not forget the other necessary critical ingredients however—her process also included nearly every component of creativity introduced in this chapter (and numerous universal skills as well): without skill at the piano, her work would not have gotten off the ground; without significant breadth of knowledge in her field of piano playing, she would not know where to artfully diverge; she had to create parameters to include some ideas and exclude others; she had to experiment to see what worked and what didn't; she liberally used the theme and variation process that included harvesting aspects of ideas and practices found in the past, such as the prepared piano, used well before her by John Cage;

she applied hard work and focus to create and pull off her innovative ideas; diverse knowledge was required in her selection and use of digital keyboards and the minting of compositions; and clear goals were mandatory for the whole idea to take off. You see, pushing a creative project through to its fruition requires a slew of skills and lots of work! I think you will agree, the creative *process* is not magic after all—but the end result can be.

Summation: Teachers can encourage their students to start working on developing their daydreaming and pondering habits early —especially as it pertains to creative work. The steps I have detailed above are a roadmap into the creative process and can be studied and replicated by each of your students in their own unique way.

10. THEME AND VARIATION

As I mentioned above, if you could keep only one idea in mind to foster creativity, theme and variation should be it. This aspect of the creative process will serve your students better than any other and will likely give them the most options as they endeavor to expand their creative potential.

Theme and variation—a technique commonly used by legions of the very best composers and other creative artists—is based upon one simple premise: take an existing idea or entity, such as a melody, a car, or a garment, and make changes to it in some way. Those changes, students are surprised to know, are usually incremental. And while making those small changes, it is important to maintain a *connecting thread* to the original idea. Once students grasp this concept, help them begin to see the instances of theme and variation at work all around them. For example, many automobiles, such as the Ford Mustang or Volkswagen Beetle, retain their same basic and recognizable shape for decades, despite innumerable tweaks. Necktie design remains basically the same year in and year out, yet ties constantly change in width. While most handbags have the same basic components—pouch, enclosure hardware, and strap—designers still manage to create endless variants of them. And even though most product designs are riffs on existing ideas, design teams made up of extremely gifted people still labor hard to come up with those changes! The reason? The precise recipe (variation amalgam!) is only accessible through the right combination of small (and very specific) variations. Yet all those creative changes (found in automobiles, neckties, handbags, etc.) employ one dominant process: theme and variation.

Impress upon your students the idea that embracing the theme and variation process is the secret to unleashing their own creative powers! Students do not need to invent something entirely new (as they often mistakenly think) to be highly creative in their music-making process (or anywhere else). The exercise below shows how a student can begin applying the theme and variation process to help them see how it works and to begin using it widely throughout their lives. Specifically, it is a method to expose a *process* which is often a primary component of creativity and used by composers throughout the centuries.

Bridge Exercise: To be clear, *compositional* variation is used here as a bridge exercise to get to *interpretational* variation. I have found that students are most comfortable in their first attempts experimenting with the theme and variation concept of creativity if they use simple, well-known melodies such as "Twinkle, Twinkle Little Star." Give students a week-long assignment, during which time they must see how many variations they can create by making one *simple* change at a time to that tune. For example, the initial rhythm in "Twinkle, Twinkle Little Star" is carried by straight quarter notes; for a variation, the student could make a single change to the melody by using a dotted rhythm, adding grace notes, or putting it into a minor key. To add another layer of possibilities to the variation process, different accompaniment patterns could be added to the melody and so on. In each example, some change takes place, but the basic melodic framework remains the same. Students will soon catch on to this theme and variation process and see it as a wonderful platform from which to springboard their own creative energies into interpretations of the pieces they are playing or in other aspects of their lives as well.

Transition: Once students become comfortable with the compositional use of theme and variation, they can transfer the technique to musical interpretation to enhance expressive creativity. This step is not quite as obvious as the latter, but very necessary because it allows the student to start crafting interpretations in the music they are practicing and performing. Demonstrating imaginative and distinctive musicianship will take more than even fingers, good tone, accurate performance practice, full dynamic range, and well-shaped phrasing—every good musician has attained those basic and essential qualities. This next step uses the theme and variation approach to stimulate creativity in the components used in interpretive expression.

Exercise: There is significant latitude for the variation of any musical component. Use this series of questions to help your student get started utilizing them in their practice and performance. What if, for example, the performance practice aspect of a piece was nudged slightly out of its accepted orbit? Why not try changing that nice full tone to something that might be more angular or flinty to help set off a change in mood or character? Why not change levels of articulation (attack) and mood in repeats to create more diversity for the listener? What if the phrasing was not always so cliché (dynamics starting softer, rising in the middle and falling again at the end) but somewhat different—maybe even slightly unusual? How many variants of pedal levels (full, half, quarter, flutter, etc.) can they use to create new effects and color changes in their playing? What if a student used this variation approach to help them create clearer divisions of range and nuance in their overall use of dynamics?

Continuing the idea of using variation to help your students' creative ability in their musical self-expression, here are some more questions to spark their imaginations: How can the speed and dynamics of an extended trill be varied in order to keep the listen's attention? How much can the width and speed of vibrato be varied? What about varying the intensity and color of the tone? All of these ideas, of course, must happen with musical intention.

In my teaching, I have found that introducing the idea of theme and variation as it applies to interpretation can be a very successful approach to helping students discover new dimensions of expression in their playing. Theme and variation, as a technique to be used in practice and performance, has become a tool my students now use to help them expand their interpretational possibilities. As students' expressive abilities increase, they also start thinking about how they might distinguish their interpretation from others. By doing so, they begin to find their own individual voice.

Summation: Using the theme and variation model, students will become more comfortable with a major component of the creative process—making incremental changes to existing elements—and begin to realize that creativity is not something genetic, impenetrable, or intangible after all. To be very clear: students can't use variation any old way in designing an interpretation. Their choices must first be directed by some element of musical awareness, experience, or sophistication. To illuminate how some of the greatest creative musical geniuses have employed theme and variation in some of their greatest musical utterances, encourage students to listen to and study works like Beethoven's Fifth Symphony or Brahms' "Variations and Fugue on a Theme by Handel" for piano. These works epitomize the art of variation at the highest levels.

In summary, learning to identify and practice compositional variation (an important form of creativity in composing) is a helpful bridge exercise to learn how to identify and practice interpretational variation (an important form of creativity in musical expression). In other words, you can teach the creative art of varying expressive devices in music.

III. PIVOT CHORD
Prepare to Transpose the Skill to a Non-Music Application

As your students become comfortable using the components of creativity in music performance (breadth of knowledge, defined parameters, experimentation, theme and variation, focus, etc.), introduce them to the importance and benefits of transferring this universal skill to non-music applications. Here, we prepare to apply the ten steps for creativity in music to a non-music area. You might ask your students how creativity could play a role in their everyday lives. Or, how might a component of the creative process (experimentation) play a role in helping them better manage the demands of their busy daily schedules or after-school job? How might the components of the creative process (such as theme and variation or defining parameters) benefit music students planning to go into a non-music career—such as building a successful business after college or distinguishing themselves while working for a company or at a university?

As mentioned in all chapters in this teaching manual, students generally don't transfer universal skills (first learned through music) to non-music applications on their own without your help. The transposed musician, however, has learned to transfer ("transpose") their universal skills consciously, confidently, and effectively from music to a new area, and in doing so with intention, bring their universal skills to a higher level and to new places in life.

As we know so well, a great many of our students do not go on to become professional musicians and yet, creative skills will most assuredly be an asset to them in non-music professions. How

233

important is it for us, then, to make sure the work we so carefully develop and craft in our students for music application is not lost when they graduate or move into non-music disciplines? I think it is very important. It turns the music lesson into a very different creature if this transference idea becomes a part of the overall teaching philosophy. Additionally, the creativity skill in music will be further strengthened as your student cross-trains that skill outside the field of music.

IV. TRANSPOSITION
Actively Transpose the Skill to a Non-Music Application

Using the same steps as in the music examples, here are some brief, non-music application examples to help guide you with ideas for transferring the creativity skill steps. Each of these ten steps may stand alone or be combined as you wish.

1. LITTLE CREATIVITY CAN BE GENERATED WITHOUT SOME SKILL LEVEL

Remind students that a certain proficiency level is needed in the area in which they wish to be creative. The higher the proficiency level the greater the creative possibilities. For example, little creativity would be possible in designing new software without some background in writing code. What could be accomplished in a chemistry lab without some foundational knowledge?

Exercise: For any student still a bit skeptical, ask them to try doing something creative in an area or field about which they know nothing. This will make it perfectly clear that skill and knowledge are needed before real creativity can begin—and hopefully create a good laugh in the process.

2. BREADTH OF KNOWLEDGE WITHIN FIELD

Knowing some history about a particular field really helps in the creative effort. How could an architect really expect to create a unique building design if she has no knowledge of existing buildings? If your student wants to build a rover vehicle for an engineering obstacle competition, learning all he could about the successes and failures of past designs would provide invaluable information on how to start building a redesigned vehicle.

Exercise: Perhaps your music student has a high school English project that involves writing a short story. What do they plan to write about? Maybe they have some interest in horses and wanted to write a story about harness racing. Some research on the subject, as supportive structure to their creative effort, would be quite beneficial to the overall credibility and believability of the story.

3. DEFINE PARAMETERS

Music students are accustomed to dealing with parameters because of the numerous dictates of the score (often "assisted" by the caring admonitions of their teachers!). Even so, musicians create very distinct interpretations all while still remaining faithful to the composer's intentions. Performers continually define and impose parameters around what they can and cannot do regarding style, performance practice, etc. Non-music disciplines are equally benefited by parameters. For example, if your student is also an athlete and wants to be competitive in running, she would need to create a training program loaded with pre-determined parameters on what to and what not to do regarding diet, workout intensity and duration, practice routines, etc.

Exercise: If your piano student is also a runner on her high-school track team, ask her to make a detailed list of what she will and will not be doing regarding her training regimen. How many parameters can she come up with that are germane and effective to the kind of running she will be doing? Times, distances, intensities, rest-periods, etc., would be a start. How much will her high school track coach provide and how much can she add on her own?

4. EXPERIMENTATION

Sometimes the path forward is not always clear. Take, for example, a college French horn player who learned to continuously experiment with modulating his sound by feathering dynamics and intonation to achieve a perfect blend in his school orchestra's brass section.

Exercise: You ask this student: how can his experimentation with blending sound be applied to his non-music job as a general concept? Through applying the idea of transference, this horn student applies the same process of subtle blending as a tactic in his new job. There, he has to work with a fellow co-worker who has a prickly personality and, consequently, experiments with "modulating" his interactions with the co-worker in order to minimize conflict and benefit their projects.

5. HARD WORK AND FOCUS

Most music students soon get a pretty good idea about what it takes to make sustained progress at a musical instrument. Coming up with a creative idea is one thing; turning it into reality is another. For a piano student, audiating the way they want to interpret a Chopin Ballade is one thing; getting it to sound that way at the piano is another. Your students will be faced with many challenges outside the field of music, also requiring creative solutions and sustained effort. In those situations, remind them to call upon and apply the experience they gained from taking a difficult piece from start to performance. Hopefully, if students begin a creative project with more awareness of the work ahead, then perhaps they will have more fortitude to stick with it and see it through.

Exercise: Have your students compare one of their biggest accomplishments in mastering a difficult piece (and what it took to arrive at that level—including all the highs and lows, successes and failures) to an important project they are involved with at school. Are they putting similar effort and thought into that project? Are they feeling like the task requires too much effort? Has their motivation flagged, and do they feel like quitting? Perhaps alerting your students to the fact that they have already made such a journey previously (mastering a difficult piece and successfully navigating all the hurdles that accompanied that journey) will help them see that their school project is not as formidable or out of reach as they previously imagined and that it is more of a familiar, repeatable process...one that they have already achieved multiple times in music.

6. DIVERSE KNOWLEDGE

As your students first learned in the music application for creativity, the creative process in one field can be enhanced by having an awareness of how the same skill is applied in another field—the idea of intersectionality. This was something the 3-M Company (a leading U.S. company with a considerable record of patents) understood and applied years ago: it had a policy that required employees from different departments of the company to mingle on a regular basis to share ideas with one another on how they approached shared challenges.

With that same idea in mind, what if a former music student of yours went on to a career in which they needed to give numerous presentations and reports—would it be helpful for them to attend some theater productions to observe how actors employ stage presence, clarity of enunciation, expression, projection, and emotion? Absolutely! And let's not forget that your prior music student could also draw upon their past experiences of successfully communicating musical ideas.

Exercise: Ask your student if they can recall any aspect of their own music drills (etudes, scales, interval practice, etc.) that could be transferred beneficially to a non-music application? Perhaps your high school student has an after-school job where they work at the take-out window of a fast-food establishment—might it be beneficial if they were to create some drill of their own (based upon their own music practice) in order to become better at something they do repetitively? Maybe it is to become more physically efficient juggling orders, making change, and talking all at the same time—something that could be practiced at home, away from work.

7. CLEAR GOALS

Most students will probably nod vigorously when you remind them just how important it is to keep goals clear when engaged in *any* important project or creative activity, not just music. In this step, impress upon students that there will be many projects in life and work where developing and maintaining clear goals are key to completing and doing them well—just as they did in putting together the goals that ultimately led them to play a successful recital.

Exercise: To help define clear goals and keep students on track on their next school project or job task, here are four simple goal-related steps for them to keep in mind no matter what work lies before them:

a. Define what you want to accomplish

b. Define how you wish to do it

c. Establish a time frame (often neglected)

d. Stick to your plan (use a calendar or journal to help assist)

8. REVERSE ENGINEERING

As we have learned, this stage includes closely examining an existing object or process to learn how it is put together or done. Much can be learned from this approach. Remind your student that any item or process is basically a lesson waiting to begin, but only if the student examines it carefully and takes care to be fully aware while doing so. If so, that awareness becomes an extraordinary learning tool because of what it can reveal to the student. Reverse engineering is also very much about keen perception. Remind your student that when they closely watch and listen to their favorite performer to learn something about a piece of music, they can apply that same observational ability to almost anything with the same depth of focus. Perhaps a student is scheduled to give a book report to their class, and they are worried they may not speak well or stumble on their words. Ask them what example of good speaking is immediately available to them for study. (Hint: national TV newscasters.) Let students know that by listening to seasoned news announcers and emulating their delivery style, speed, rhythm, and clarity, they will have picked up a great deal about effective speaking through the process of reverse engineering.

Exercise: Have your student take an item apart that they have little-to-no knowledge of. Perhaps you suggest something such as an old clock or a discarded pair of jeans. If it happens to be the jeans, their job is to take them apart seam by seam to figure out how various sections and seams are put together and sewn. For example, how is the wide, thicker seam folded together in order to make such a seam? How many rows of stitching were required? How does that seam contrast with the one on the opposite side of the leg? By engaging in this reverse engineering exercise, the student realizes just how much information is available to them if they make the effort to look closely enough or, if necessary, physically deconstruct something. It is an immensely helpful exercise. Once the student completes a simple reverse engineering experiment, the next time this sort of scrutiny is needed the process may not seem nearly as foreign or off-putting.

9. DAYDREAMING

When do our students actually give their minds free rein to surf about unfettered and explore without interruption or demand? It probably doesn't happen often, especially in their jam-packed, overly scheduled lives. Perhaps we might suggest to our students that they start by sometimes reducing the constant demands they place upon their minds and time. That they should strongly consider giving themselves a rest period or two each day where they make no demands upon themselves and just let their minds relax and wander. Give them permission! What results might such an exercise produce? I have heard many people report on the importance and success of daydreaming. What non-music task or project might a music student have that requires creativity? Perhaps they are confronted by a problem that requires creating a makeshift tool to provide a fix to something. Suggesting that they let their minds roam to help search for a creative solution is surely a start. Creative people have learned to maximize their daydreaming time and do not think of it as wasted.

They go about it willingly, eagerly, and give their minds total freedom to snoop about in all the nooks and crannies. They also are open to possibilities, dismissing nothing, and remaining in the moment. "Daydreaming" can be considered the mind's incubator. When we're hyper-focused, the possibility of the mind wandering about in its vast reservoir and finding an "Aha!" diminishes. In daydreaming, as Will Willimon said in a recent Time article, there's no controlling sensor to whisper "That's ridiculous" or "That's completely impractical."[11] So, by all means, take some time to do away with that self-imposed mental censor whose sole reason for being seems to be to limit possibilities.

Here, in the non-music application, encourage students to allow their minds to wander and daydream when faced with a challenging situation when a creative solution is needed. Remind them to begin this process by sitting still in a quiet place or just quietly walking along a nature path. Then, encourage your students to purposely consider solutions that don't seem main-stream or obvious. To help acclimate them to that notion, try the following exercise.

Exercise: Ask a student this: if one arm on a pair of glasses lost its attaching screw, how many different ways could the glasses be repaired back to functional form in an emergency without using a screw? This could be an assignment for the following week. To help them come up with possible answers, suggest that they try letting their mind wander. See how many inventive solutions your student can come up with, i.e., could they use a pocketknife to whittle a twig down to just the right thickness to work like the screw to allow the hinge to function? Could the student use a wire twister or a piece of thread hanging from a hem to re-attach the arm of the glasses?

10. THEME AND VARIATION

Remind your student that they needn't feel like they have to come up with something entirely new to be creative. Quite the opposite! Take well-known existing items and make small variations to them to change or improve their function.

Exercise: In this example, your music student works in a store where she has been asked to "dress" the window. She tells you that she is overwhelmed at the prospect of having to present the store's latest spring fashions on five mannequins in an eye-catching exhibit. You ask her to recall her theme and variation discussion from a past music lesson with you—that composers often meter out small changes at a time to a melody, rhythm, and harmony. After a bit of thinking, she realized that she could transfer this theme and variation concept to her work in the store. There, she knows that each mannequin's position and apparel would merely need to be a variant of the one next to it—each one did not have to look dramatically different from the others in order to make an effective display. Perhaps a flashy scarf here, a trendy belt there, or a different color of trousers on another is all that would be needed to differentiate one mannequin from the other and complete the work to her employer's satisfaction.

In summary, you can dramatically help your students just by planting seeds—using these skill transference suggestions and exercises. Not all are going to germinate right away. Some will take hold and others may take time to become beneficial. You can choose as much or as little time as you wish to devote to this transference stage—see how your student responds and understands.

V. RECAP
Revisit Skill in Music

Now that your students have exercised some (or all) of these creativity steps in both music and non-music applications, remind them that it can "circle back" to further inform them about improving its application in music. Here's an example. Perhaps you have a high school piano student who is very much interested in studying biomechanics in college. When you introduced to him the concept of reverse-engineering applied through music he didn't really take to it, but he loved applying the idea to objects around him. He was soon taking apart every mechanical device he could find to see how each one worked. After doing this for a while, it finally became clear to him how much his piano playing would benefit if only he would apply his love of reverse-engineering to music with the same conviction. (You had long wanted him to carefully listen to YouTube performances of great pianists playing Chopin so he could develop a better sense of rubato.)

This example shows how one application of a skill can benefit another—either going from the music application to the non-music application or vice-versa. We won't always know from which direction the benefit will come, but usually it will. That is the beauty of the transference process: cross-training a universal skill in diverse applications forms a well-learned lesson. It reinforces the idea that extraordinary lessons are available to us everywhere and at almost every moment if we but make the connections and practice them.

VI. QUESTIONS FOR REFLECTION

1. Has your perception of creativity changed or been modified? Do you believe that aspects of it can be taught?
2. How have your students responded to ideas on how to improve their creativity?
3. Do your students see beneficial relationships between music applications and non-music applications?
4. Which of the ten creativity components has proven to be more successful or popular in your studio?

VII. SUGGESTED READING

Baer, John. *Creativity and Divergent Thinking*. (Hillsdale, NJ: Lawrence Erlbaum Associates, Publishers, 1993).

Barth, Diane. *Daydreaming: Unlock the Creative Power of Your Mind*. (London, UK: Penguin Books, 1998).

Csíkszentmihályi, Mihály. *Creativity: The Psychology of Discovery and Invention*. (New York, New York: Harper Perennial, 1996).

Kaufman, Barry S., and Gregoire, Carolyn. *Wired to Create: Unraveling the Mysteries of the Creative Mind*. (New York, New York: Penguin Random House LLC, 2016).

Kaufman, James C., and Sternberg, Robert J. *The Cambridge Handbook of Creativity*. (New York, NY: Cambridge University Press, 2010).

Johansson, Frans. *The Medici Effect: What Elephants and Epidemics Can Teach Us About Innovation*. (Boston, MA: Harvard Business Review Press, 2017).

Maisel, Eric. *The Creativity Book, A Year's Worth of Inspiration and Guidance.* (New York, NY: Jeremy P. Tarcher/Putnam, 2000).

Ristad, Eloise. *A Soprano on Her Head.* (Moab, UT: Real People Press, 1982).

Savage, Dylan. *How to Teach Creativity in the Music Lesson.* Clavier Companion, digital only, September, 2018.

Savage, Dylan. *What Are We Learning in Piano Study?* Clavier Companion, September/October, 2018, p. 46

VIII. REFERENCES

1. John Daido Loori, *The Zen of Creativity: Cultivating Your Artistic Life.* (New York, New York: Ballantine Books, 2005), 1.

2. Austin Kleon, *Steal Like An Artist.* (New York, New York: Workman Publishing Company, Inc., 2012), 7.

3. Tom and David Kelly, *Confidence: Unleashing the Creative Potential Within Us All.* (New York, NY: Crown Business, 2013), 22.

4. Ecclesiastes, 1:9. The Holy Bible, Revised Standard Version. (Cleveland OH: The World Publishing Company, 1963), 587.

5. The New Oxford American Dictionary. 2nd edition. (New York, NY: Oxford University Press, 2005), 196.

6. Gregory J Feist, "The Function of Personality in Creativity," from *The Cambridge Handbook of Creativity,* edited by James C. Kaufman and Robert J. Sternberg, 113–30. Cambridge Handbooks in Psychology (Cambridge: Cambridge University Press, 2010), 113-4.

7. Johanna Keller, *Yo-Yo Ma's Edge Effect.* The Chronicle Review, March 23, 2007.

8. Frans Johansson, *The Medici Effect: What Elephants and Epidemics Can Teach Us About Innovation.* (Boston, MA: Harvard Business Review Press, 2006), 5.

9. Jonah Lehrer, *The Virtues of Daydreaming,* New Yorker, Annals of Technology, June 5, 2012.

10. Kathleen Supové, www.supove.com (accessed 6-24-18)

11. Will Willimon. *The Importance of Daydreaming,* Time, May 23, 2014.

IX. NOTES

CHAPTER 9

BENEFITS TO TEACHERS, MUSIC SCHOOLS, AND DEPARTMENTS

In this book, I have illustrated how to teach universal skills as a primary focus in the music lesson. Again, the difference between the traditional music lesson and this method of systematically teaching universal skills within the traditional music lesson is that in this system the following steps are observed: a.) you teach your student the specific skill steps in music; b.) the student practices them in music with conscious awareness; c.) you coach them to actively transfer the steps to a new area in their life. This cross-training further imbeds the musical version of the steps by providing a deeper understanding through an alternative, non-music experience.

I hope that using these processes to expand the current purpose and scope of music study will prove intriguing and helpful to students and teachers alike. Music teachers have long expressed that their students, in the process of studying music, use universal skills such as problem-solving, collaboration, and creativity along the way. However, unless those universal skills are taught systematically and applied comprehensively, the learning of those skills is mainly left to chance, with the student largely trying to figure them out and improve them on their own.

This book, then, is the first to provide a systematic method for an active and comprehensive study of universal skills through the traditional music lesson. Teachers will be able to make a case that when these universal skills are defined, learned, applied in the music lesson, and then actively transferred to all areas of life, students will have the potential to receive significant benefits beyond what the traditional lesson provides. In summation, the goal of this book is to improve students' performance levels, not only at their instrument, but in *all* aspects of life.

Even for the most talented music students, thorough universal skill learning is an important component to add to the music lesson because it allows them to maximize their capabilities at their instrument. High-level playing requires superb problem-solving, communication, creativity, focus, critical thinking, and more. Musicians contemplating a career in music must now have entrepreneurial and interdisciplinary capabilities in addition to extraordinary performance skills—all of which can be greatly enhanced by universal skills.

The benefits of universal skill training are unassailable—precisely why they are so highly touted by educators and business leaders throughout the world. These skills are even more necessary to musicians than ever. According to the highly regarded and comprehensive Strategic National Arts Alumni Project (SNAAP) 2016 annual report, "Artists frequently work intermittently, hold more than one job at once, and/or alternate between arts- and non-arts-related employment."[1] In addition, the report also states that "among alumni who currently or previously have worked as artists, the likelihood of working across disciplines has been consistently high..."[2] (The SNAAP study includes all arts categories.)

Finding accurate data to back up the anecdotal evidence or hunches we have regarding the careers music students acquire after they graduate has been difficult to find prior to the SNAAP survey. The reason: partly, perhaps, because music schools (and other arts-related schools and programs) may be hesitant, for obvious reasons, to reveal the actual percentages of their students able to make a living in the profession for which they were trained. Thankfully, we now have real numbers; the SNAAP 2015 & 2016 Aggregate Frequency Report shows only 11% of musicians with undergraduate and 27% with graduate degrees are employed full-time in the field of music.[3] Those are very low percentages indeed, and support what most of us already know: making a living as a musician is quite difficult, due to many factors. Although we music teachers may not have had actual data on the music employment rates of our students before the SNAAP study, we already knew they were quite low. I know many of us have pondered the disparity in the amount of time, effort, and money needed to become a good, competent musician versus the actual success rate of making a living at it. I believe we owe it to our students to prepare them as well and fully as possible to forge a livelihood that may, or even more likely, may not include music.

Most of us have been taught in the Western European Conservatory model of music training, the one which advocates maximizing instrument proficiency as the sole focus. Its overriding purpose: learn to play as well as possible with artist-level teachers and the rest will take care of itself. I believe this model has long been outdated and needs to be adjusted, but certainly not wholly discontinued. For the vast majority of our students, a new music lesson model is needed— and I invite you to consider the one presented in this book, in which universal skills are part of the fundamental approach. Since a vast majority of our students will not make a living in music (even though music will most likely remain an important and meaningful part of their lives), why not use the music lesson, instead, as a primary vehicle to help improve their chances for success in other disciplines? I know this idea is a major shift in the current thinking, but keep in mind that a majority of the eight universal skills presented in this book are at the top of the lists that business and university leaders often say students and employees need most. Being more adept at using these universal skills will be extremely helpful, no matter what the application.

What parent of a K-12 student, after recognizing the potential of *The Transposed Musician* music lessons, in which universal skill learning is the primary focus, would not want such lessons for their children? Instead of instrument proficiency being the top priority, universal skill learning could be the co-priority or even *the* priority itself. The balance between the two in the lesson would be up to the teacher and the student. Instead of solely using the old European Conservatory model of teaching, why not change the direction of the music lesson just a little? I think many music teachers and professors will find this possibility quite exciting and at the same time, relieving—knowing that they are providing their students a set of defined skills with universal application.

With the demand for universal skills so high, this book can help music teachers to be in a better position to demonstrate just how well and how many of these skills can be taught through the study of an instrument. This repurposing and reimagining of the traditional music lesson gives the platform of music advocacy renewed energy and opens new possibilities for research in the potential benefits of using applied music study to benefit careers in non-music disciplines. Of course, instilling a life-long love of music and deepening a sense of aesthetics and culture will always be a priority in the music lesson— this is not in question.

DOES RECRUITING SOMETIMES BENEFIT THE TEACHER IN THE MUSIC DEPARTMENT OR SCHOOL MORE THAN THE STUDENT?

This question is directed to those of us in higher education and may be a difficult (and touchy) question to answer. (It continues along a topic I broached in the introduction.) As documented in the SNAAP reports above, careers in music are very hard to develop and the percentage of graduating musicians who end up supporting themselves in music careers is quite low. My book, in part, is a response to my own thinking on this subject and the questions I have asked myself often over the last two decades: Who am I helping most, my own teaching career or my students? What am I helping my students prepare for? How can I best help them? How aware of the changing times and music-marketplace am I and how can I best adapt as a teacher? For a long time, I have been wholly convinced that systematic and thorough universal skills training in the music lesson is vitally important and a substantial answer to those questions. For that reason, I do not teach any other way. Every lesson includes an introduction or review of a necessary universal skill. If a student is still struggling with practice efficiency, I will review problem-solving and focus steps. If my student struggles with a tendency to rush through the learning process and miss details, I may start by helping them with tips on patience. And, I always make sure to connect the skill's use to a purpose outside the field of music, too. I might ask, "Could you use patience to benefit a friendship or, perhaps, even yourself? How might communication skills benefit your next job interview? How might applying well-honed problem-solving skills better help a big life decision such as creating a career that embraces all your particular strengths? For me, the systematic learning, application, and transference of universal skills in the music lesson is always a priority.

In addition to the music and life benefits students gain from learning and applying universal skills, I hope this method will help provide some answers to teachers regarding the lingering questions I addressed in the paragraph above. I know I am not alone in this thinking after having spoken with numerous college and university music colleagues over the years. The overriding question for me was: considering how few traditional music jobs and opportunities actually exist in the music marketplace, how could I in good faith continue to recruit music students into my studio and department? My solution was the teaching method I developed and have set forth in this book. As most college music faculty know, the recruiting task is becoming increasingly difficult: we are shaking more bushes and looking under more rocks in order to populate our programs with qualified students. Why is that? Are music students becoming more aware of the reality regarding what lies ahead after graduation? You are certainly not alone if you have asked yourself if you are primarily recruiting for the preservation of your job. Yes, recruiting has always been a part of any applied teacher's university position, but right now it seems more challenging and problematic than ever. It's one thing to go after top talent (not forgetting the fact that substantial scholarship offers can often be among the most effective enticements). It is quite another thing to struggle to merely populate the studio with warm bodies. In my conversations with colleagues, the latter situation is where many college and university applied music professors increasingly find themselves. The ethical dilemma of recruiting music students to fill studios when there is little-to-no possibility for employment in their field is no longer a "hidden subject"—something I mentioned in the introduction, citing two prominent piano professors, Robert Weirich and Yoheved Kaplinsky.

Germane to this conversation, I think most music teachers, not just college applied music faculty, will welcome a teaching method which helps address this difficult issue and provides a mitigating path out of the dilemma increasingly exacerbated by continuing the old, Western European Conservatory style of teaching music. What if our new path of using applied music to cross-train universal skills was designed to become a springboard for some of our incoming music students who, ultimately, may have other career plans, helping them acquire expert-level universal skills that will benefit them when they eventually become doctors, educators, lawyers, or scientists? What would music programs look like if that was a *primary purpose*? Would we be doing more good that way than preparing legions of musicians, in the traditional way, for careers that largely don't exist? I certainly think so! Imagine a music department website stating, "Come study music here, we'll help prepare you to become better doctors, scientists, and teachers!" While this would mean a considerable shift in direction—and may seem way out in left field for some—I see it as a viable, ethical, and sustainable possibility for maintaining and growing student populations, especially in music departments that struggle to maintain their numbers or face declining student enrollment.

WHAT IF WE DO NOTHING AND CONTINUE ON OUR OLD, FAMILIAR PATH?

Think about the current climate in music performance fields and where this all may lead in the next decade or two. Will it include the mass closing or drastic restructuring of music degree programs? Will retiring applied music professors just not be replaced? I now see, with more regularity, full-time, tenure-track music faculty positions that do not continue after a professor retires (throughout my state and the nation). Remember the College Music Society's eye-catching pre-conference workshop topic in the 2016 national conference called "The End of the Conservatory" (mentioned in the introduction of this book)? That topic did not come out of the blue; college music administrators are well aware that adjustments to the 19th century European Conservatory model are critical to the creation of thriving 21st century music schools and departments and those changes need to be addressed now.

UNIVERSAL SKILLS ARE HOT TOPICS FOR A REASON

Not surprisingly, the eight universal skills mentioned in this book are the very ones state legislators and board members recognize and value, partly because so many of them are business people who require these skills among their employees or staff. Why not use the fertile ground of the music lesson to help students indelibly learn these very skills for a broader purpose? After all, what discipline requires as many universal skills and at such levels as music performance? Wouldn't state legislators—the very ones who control the purse strings of all state university systems throughout the U.S.—be very interested to hear that music departments and schools are starting to use universal skill-building as a new foundation of their music programs? What if those programs were developed not only for the purpose of helping graduating music students become more job versatile and capable, but had similar options for students majoring in other disciplines throughout the university as well?

The student who learns to express themselves and communicate well through their instrument, for example, by using universal principles of communication skills *and who is taught how to transfer those principles to other fields* is in a position to be more marketable to jobs requiring good communication skills. That same student will now be able to confidently and successfully promote their ideas while speaking to a room full of people (having already been prepared in the music lesson to use principles of rhetoric and having tested them in numerous performances in front of audiences). That student would also be quite accustomed to and skilled working as a collaborator, having exercised teamwork skills in countless ensemble rehearsals and performances throughout their earlier years—skills that can then be transferred with conscious intent to any instance involving group decision-making.

ADDED VALUE

Now that you have shown your students (and their parents) the benefits of applying universal skills to music making and to life, it is time to consider (yes!) the increased business *you* may receive from offering parents the option of their children learning *The Transposed Musician* approach. Like any other business, you can expand your studio offerings (product line!) by providing this method as an option. Or, maybe, you will offer it solely as your new approach. In purely business terms, a new product can increase the bottom line. You can view the universal skill learning and transference component of the lesson as another "product" in the education you provide. Offering this added value component is not only a way to increase the number of students in your studio, but it may also enable you to increase your lesson fee if skill transference is part of the package. Now, not only will Veronica learn to play the piano and develop a love for music, but the lessons she takes will also include consistent, comprehensive universal skill training and transference—which can benefit her in any discipline she chooses, be it STEM, education, medicine, law, etc. What parent won't immediately see the value in that?

A WILD IDEA!

The ideas found in *The Transposed Musician* may even inspire music teachers to increase the scope and purpose of their studio to attract students who aren't interested in traditional music lessons at all, but who *would* be interested in the idea of learning, through music, a comprehensive universal skill program that will benefit them later in college and beyond. What if there were a whole segment of students for whom learning to play an instrument became the secondary purpose for the lesson, using it, instead, as a vehicle for developing high level universal skills to be used in other careers? This new twist on the purpose of the music lesson could provide teachers a whole new range of possibilities. What would your music lessons look like then? I encourage you to find out! Of course, there is no one way to do this. Trust your instincts. What could be more satisfying than knowing you are providing your students with universal skills that can function at a level far beyond the intent of the traditional lesson?

And, which will simultaneously benefit their instrument skill at the same time? Interestingly, the skills I have detailed in this book will be some of the very ones you will need to use in your exploration!

FOR PARENTS QUESTIONING THE VALUE OF MUSIC LESSONS

As we know, some parents do not see much value in the traditional music lesson. In such instances, perhaps focusing on the skill transference component of the lesson might just be the added "value" some parents will need to make the commitment to enroll their children in music lessons. The deciding factor in that decision may come after you have clearly explained the idea and benefits of transference to them—making the connection between skills first learned in the music lesson and their benefit to non-music disciplines. It would be a great idea to let parents know that college and university admission directors highly value student applicants who mention that they have a music background. Medical schools, for example, are filled with top-performing students who have had music backgrounds. To help parents gather source material along those lines, ask them to visit the website of the Kaufman Music Center,[4] a long-time and highly successful community music school in New York City. There, they will find lists of studies that help back up the claims that the study of music can greatly benefit students in non-music disciplines.

Additionally, teaching music lessons in order to predominantly enrich and benefit lives outside the field of music is certainly not a new concept. In her book *Making Music and Enriching Lives*, music teacher Bonnie Blanchard advocates that very concept in her approach called "Music for Life,"[5] which prioritizes pride, respect, relationships, commitment to excellence, love of learning, positive attitude, and so on. These are also important and vital components for life (like universal skills) that teachers and music departments could consider developing in their curriculums.

BE DIRECT WITH THOSE WHO ARE STEADFAST IN SEEKING A CAREER IN MUSIC

We need to mention, even to our most music career-oriented students (if you haven't already), just how difficult and competitive a career in music can be; only a small percentage of musicians reach a competitive, professional level competency. And even then, within that group, only a few musicians actually get to a point where they can support themselves as a professional. As we know, music degrees such as the BA, BM, and MM do not guarantee any level of success in music as a career, and a DMA does not guarantee a job in academe—yet many students (and their parents) do not know this. But the heads of music departments and schools know! Joe Robinson, former Principal Oboist of the New York Philharmonic and Chair of an Advisory Board for Oberlin Conservatory, commented two decades ago on the grave situation facing music school performance graduates, "I think there is a great deal of concern among music school deans and conservatory presidents about this."[6] Others have agreed: Richard Nass, former English horn in the Metropolitan Opera (on advising students wanting to pursue a music performance career) said "Only do this if you cannot conceive of doing anything else, and do it without the idea of making money doing it."[7] I am reminded again of Yoheved Kaplinsky of the Juilliard School counseling her prospective piano students not to consider a music career unless they can't imagine doing anything else.[8] All three comments show that this is not a new condition in the state of our field!

WHAT WILL MUSIC LESSONS LOOK LIKE IN THE FUTURE?

I wish to state again: I do not think we need to dissolve the Western European Conservatory path of study. In my estimation, that great tradition of the music lesson (and accompanying coursework) will always continue. The question is, just how many schools can continue to offer this particular path *unchanged*? I feel we must add or make changes to that tradition whenever needed. And, change *is* occurring and being embraced. We only need to look at the fairly recent inclusion (in the last few decades) of all the wellness and entrepreneurship classes appearing in music schools and departments throughout the country to see that happening. Those two course topics did not exist before the early eighties. Now those courses are not only popular, but sometimes required to graduate. I offer the following, very brief examples of the genesis of those two topics (and my involvement in them) only to help back up a prediction I make below.

It was people like Alice Brandfonbrener, a pioneer in the field of music wellness, who started the first annual Symposium on the Medical Problems of Musicians in Aspen, Colorado in 1983, whom we have to thank for starting one of these new and much-needed areas of examination in the field of music. (Her organization is still going strong and now known as PAMA—Performing Arts Medicine Association.) I was privileged to be a faculty member in that performing arts medicine symposium in 1987 and 1988, where I debuted my research on slow-motion analysis of arm, hand, and finger movement at the keyboard to reduce injury and increase proficiency. (My work was later published in Clavier Magazine.[9]) Now, wellness for musicians programs are found throughout music departments and schools.

At the same time music entrepreneurship was just being developed as a program for musicians at the University of Colorado-Boulder in the early-to-mid eighties (one of the first in the country), I had already created a business called Sound Health Innovations, now called What's Music Got To Do With It, in which I pioneered approaches that use live music performance to help business leaders learn high-touch creativity, focus, collaboration, and listening skills. My client list includes State Farm Insurance, VF Corporation, Lucent Technology, Eli Lilly, and others.[10] In 1996, the Indiana University School of Music accepted my proposal for two summer courses called Music Wellness and Music Entrepreneurship. (Apparently the topics were so cutting-edge and unfamiliar that enrollment was not sufficient for the class to happen!) Currently, Indiana University's Jacobs School of Music offers a certificate in entrepreneurship. I continue to speak and write nationally on the subject of music entrepreneurship.[11]

Music educators continue to look for new areas of relevance for the field of music. Now that music wellness and entrepreneurship have become fixtures in many music programs across the country, *I predict that teaching universal skills in the music lesson will become commonplace in the future as well.* In their groundbreaking 2020 book, *Beyond the Conservatory Model: Reimagining Classical Music Performance Training in Higher Education,* authors Michael Stepniak and Peter Sirotin provide a comprehensive, national survey of leading music educators and administrators who discuss ways that classical music training in higher education can better anticipate and shape the needs of our students and how our field may need to adapt in order to survive. In their chapter "Making Change That Counts," they state that "Our schools could undertake a major initiative to reshape our DMA and PhD degrees to ensure that our graduating students exit with critical skills and knowledge related to innovation and change."[12] I strongly believe that universal skill training and transference provides a much-needed solution to fulfill such a major initiative and will be a major tool to meet the new demands in our field, from grade school to grad school.

No matter their career, well-learned universal skills can give *all* of your students an edge. For those supremely talented students bent on a career in music, universal skill training is just as valuable and important as it is for any other music student, because these skills are at the very heart of learning an instrument well. By teaching universal skills in the lesson, our students will gain highly functional tools to help them face the many challenges while starting to forge careers in music. Comprehensive universal skills can help them gain the creativity to dream up big, new ideas; the patience to go the necessary distance; the focus to keep goals on target; the problem-solving steps to surmount the hurdles that are invariably found along the way; the collaboration techniques to work well with others; the critical thinking acumen to successfully wade through conflicting views and information; the improvisational ability to be able to deal with the unexpected and to capitalize on the new opportunities that may arise; and the communication prowess to clearly and convincingly proclaim their ideas and projects to the world.

If widely embraced, this new direction would represent a profound shift in the way we view music lessons and how we will spend time with our students. If you think that this may be simultaneously terrifying and exhilarating, I totally agree. But, doesn't it also open up many more possibilities to broaden the purpose and viability of studying music and push our profession forward? I strongly believe teaching universal skill proficiency and transference will be vital to our students and to our field.

In conclusion, I hope I have been successful in explaining my ideas and concepts on expanding the purpose of the music lesson and how this approach has the potential to become part of the necessary evolution of the traditional music lesson. In separate chapters, I have identified and defined eight universal skills, demonstrated how to teach them comprehensively in the music lesson, given examples to show active transfer ("transposition") for their application *outside* the field of music, and finally, illustrated how those eight skills can circle back (cross-training) to further reinforce the students' musical abilities. These concepts can become a basic blueprint for use in your music lessons. My goal is to help inspire your own creative ideas for teaching universal skill application and transference in the lesson as you see fit. The level and degree to which you apply skill transference is entirely on a student-by-student basis (as their capabilities and interests allow). I hope that the ideas presented here have ignited your imagination and offer much potential for further exploration.

> — Dylan Savage
> January, 2020
> www.TheTransposedMusician.com
> www.WhatsMusicGotToDoWithIt.com

I. REFERENCES

1. Strategic National Arts Alumni Project, 2016 Annual Report, *Institutional Connections, Resources, and Working Across Disciplines: What Arts Alumni Are Saying*, www.snaap.indiana.edu/pdf/2016/SNAAP_Annual_Report_2016_FINAL.pdf, 8. (Accessed 6-15-17.)

2. Ibid, 8.

3. Strategic National Arts Alumni Project, 2015 & 2016 Aggregate Frequency Report, www.snaap.indiana.edu/pdf/2016/SNAAP15_16_Aggregate%20Report.pdf, 34. (accessed 6-15-17)

4. The Kaufman Music Center, 126 W. 67th St., New York, NY, 10023. https://www.kaufmanmusiccenter.org (accessed 11-20-19)

5. Bonnie Blanchard, *Making Music and Enriching Lives: a Guide for all Music Teachers* (Bloomington, IN: Indiana University Press, 2007), 26.

6. Nora Post, "Career Choices and Music Advocacy: Joseph Robinson Talks With Nora Post," *Double Reed* 22, (1999).

7. Ibid.

8. Yoheved Kaplinsky. "Most FAQ Regarding the Mechanics of Piano Playing." Conference Lecture, World Piano Pedagogy Conference, Anaheim, CA, 10-26-2005 (recollection of the author).

9. Dylan Savage, "What Pianists Can Learn from Athletes," *Clavier* 32, No. 9 (November 1993).

10. Dylan Savage, *What's Music Got to Do With It?*, www.whatsmusicgottodowithit.com (accessed 1-20-20).

11. Dylan Savage, "The Key to Entrepreneurship for Musicians: Marketing and Selling," *American Music Teacher* (April/May, 2008).

12. Michael Stepniak and Peter Sirotin, *Beyond the Conservatory Model: Reimagining Classical Music Performance Training in Higher Education*, *CMS Emerging Fields in Music* (New York, NY: Routledge, 2020), 102.

II. NOTES

POSTSCRIPT

In early 2020, a pandemic took over and upended our world. Almost overnight, nearly every aspect of the music world dramatically changed as well, in profound and unnerving ways, to say the very least. We have been forced into a virtual existence. Social distancing and home quarantine are anathema to our art; we normally thrive on performing, giving lessons, and attending concerts *in person*, not being separated from those experiences by digital filters. Like many musicians, I thought a lot about what impact this jarring event could have on our field in the future.

We hope against hope that things will return to the way they were but sense they may never quite get there. If so, what new world might that be? Will choirs and orchestras be able to rehearse in spaces large enough to accommodate social distancing parameters? Will venues ever be able to hold audiences in the usual close proximity and will people be willing to take health risks to hear a live performance when they can watch and listen to virtually any performer or music ensemble in the world from the comfort of their home, on HD TVs attached to high quality speakers? Will our new at-home listening habits be tough to break once the green light is given to return to concert halls? When this pandemic is finally contained or has run its course, who and what organizations will be able to survive this period financially? How will music departments and schools fare? What indelible changes will come? Will the high cost of becoming a professional musician (time, effort, money, emotion, sacrifice, etc.) seem too great, even for the most driven, when reflected against our current vast uncertainty and the ensuing changes?

These questions are not meant to create more insecurity and uncertainty, but to help remind and reinforce the fact that we musicians have always been extraordinarily resilient—even in ways we might not readily identify. For example, many of us might not realize just how ideally equipped we are to face the current crisis, monumental as it is. But we are. Take a moment to recall all the significant adversities you have overcome to become a musician. Not least among those adversities were the significant challenges posed by the years of daily struggles it took to get where you are. Yes, you are a veteran of meeting and surmounting challenges! In my thinking, that also makes you ideally suited to meet the coming challenges produced by this pandemic.

Unfortunately, the current issues in music higher education will be exacerbated as well. In many ways, the fallout from this pandemic will merely illuminate more intensely and accelerate some of the growing concerns that already exist, especially concerns with maintaining enrollment and offering relevant music courses and programs that address current music marketplace climates.

It is safe to say that long-term change will be required of us, much the same way change was required in the post-9/11 years (i.e., greatly increased security screening protocols became the new normal). For teachers and performers, the two big questions are: What will these changes be and how will we meet them? Those are questions we can't answer precisely just yet. But we can identify precisely what tools we'll need to meet the challenges posed by change; they are universal skills, including problem-solving, focus, patience, creativity, collaboration, analytical thinking, and many others. And if we are inclined a bit more now to include those skills in lessons, you now know that we as music teachers have an extremely functional and wonderful platform upon which to teach those skills at very high, comprehensive levels. Perhaps this moment is just the right time to begin.

For those still on the fence after reading this book—those who believe that comprehensive universal skill learning as a major component in the music lesson is a nice idea, but not really a necessity—I would now suggest that the current sweeping changes in our world will demand fluency in those skills even more in the coming months and years. Teaching them will also help the sustainability of our profession. To show how a different context can create a new urgency for an idea, recall that 2020 presidential candidate Andrew Yang's proposal of Universal Basic Income (UBI) scarcely caused ripples across the political spectrum. (Let's not forget to credit Dr. Martin Luther King, Jr., who proposed the same idea decades ago.) Suddenly, however, the idea of UBI is seriously considered as a necessity when framed by the gravity of tens of millions of unemployed people! Now the idea is not only seen as a viable way out of this economic calamity, but also as a long-term solution to another looming issue: the increasing use of robotics and artificial intelligence that continues to erode jobs humans perform.

In the same way, the current crisis is now producing a highly accelerated need for change in our music teaching world and may force us to reconsider what we think is important in the music lesson and to perhaps now consider what we may have shrugged at just a little bit ago. If music programs and teachers chronically attract fewer students willing to invest the vast amounts of time, energy, and sacrifice necessary to produce the proficiency required to even contemplate a professional career in music, then perhaps more teachers will see the relevance of re-orienting their music lessons in order to better benefit music and non-music careers alike. Comprehensive universal skill training fits the bill.

I have shown in previous chapters how universal skills can be comprehensively learned through the music lesson as well or better than with any other platform. I think this gives us tremendous incentive and potential upon which to capitalize—*especially* now. It can become our new niche! And we don't have to jettison our beloved Western European conservatory ideals and training. We just add to that wonderful tradition by placing universal skill training front and center in the music lesson. Why? Because those skills are such extraordinary tools with limitless applications and benefits (which, let's not forget, also significantly help musicians to practice and perform their best).

Should we now strongly consider changing our focus to better prepare more of our students for eventual blended careers or careers entirely *outside* the field of music? Yes! And I am also suggesting a new step: Why not consider imagining *entirely new careers in music* which do not yet exist—ones which would give musicians new opportunities to make a living within the field they love? I think we must try! I believe this pandemic adds new urgency to the idea of re-imagining where music may go, and this time we may be acting totally out of necessity (the mother of invention).

There are new paths we can take as musicians to augment our career possibilities. Think about a combination of performing and teaching—stuff we *already* do, just a bit differently. Then, imagine a world where musicians are employed to appear (perhaps by livestream) in almost every workplace (corporations, factories, banks, hospitals, K–12 schools, etc.). And not "solely" as performers or teachers in the traditional sense, but to use real-time music performance to teach and demonstrate important concepts and universal skills to employees, executives, and students. This variation on teaching and performing includes a new twist—teaching these concepts and skills through *our* lens to non-musicians for application in *their* fields (remember, variation is at the root of creativity). Problem-solving, focus, creativity, analytical thinking, collaboration, and others skills are all treasured in the workplace. Businesses spend fortunes to educate their workforce in those very skills. How might their needs be met by hiring a musician using *The Transposed Musician* approach?

To help spur the imagination, I am including an illustration (below) of what I think a totally different career in music might look like. In chapter nine, "Benefits to Teachers" (pg. 260), I alluded briefly to an approach I created using live music performance to help business leaders learn "high-touch" (advanced) universal skills such as creativity, focus, collaboration, etc. These ideas are based on my own experience from my consulting business, What's Music Got To Do With It? For more than 25 years I have used my own solo music performance in some very unusual ways. During those years I found that my approach has real potential for scaling up.

Here is the illustration, derived from my own professional consulting experience—something I have repeated in many settings.

Instead of the usual boring PowerPoint lecture most employees are "treated to" in their professional development sessions, they are introduced to a musician! In this particular instance, it happened to be me, when I sat on a stage in front of a Yamaha digital grand piano and a microphone in a cavernous conference space in Lancaster, PA for a national gathering of perhaps 2,000 executives and mid-level management for the VF Corporation (the fourteen-billion-dollar holding company for brands such as Lee, Wrangler, Timberland, Nautica, and Vans). This college piano professor had been hired, not to entertain, but to perform a demonstration of "continuous improvement" (a buzz phrase in the corporate world) to people in the clothing business. I was the featured presenter in the closing session of the conference—their big sendoff.

Had I been asked years earlier to give this lecture-performance, when I hadn't thought about using music performance in this way, I would have said, "Are you crazy, I can't do that—and what could I possibly say that would be of value to those folks?" Actually, I had plenty to say, because when it really comes down to it, most of us (no matter the profession) grapple with many of the same basic issues each day: confronting problems, increasing efficiency, maintaining motivation, struggling to focus, and improving collaborative skills, etc. It was only after I gave myself "permission" to really imagine a new world for myself as a musician (because I wasn't having much luck making a living wage as a concert pianist) that these ideas started to take shape and become a reality. So there I was, speaking from my heart about everything I knew about practicing to 2,000 people who were definitely not musicians. They wanted to get a different perspective on what continuous improvement (practicing!) was all about, so they could perhaps learn to improve on the things that were most important to them. By the way, when was the last time you heard about a class on the art of practicing *anything*? Our education system just doesn't include that rather critical detail.

"All" I had to do in that conference setting was to articulate specifics about my own decades of daily practice and to play sections of music (all styles, not just classical) to demonstrate process. I made sure to let my VF Corp. audience know that "important stuff" usually improves slowly and incrementally, not quickly and in big strides. I told them that I learned to love that kind of gradual pace because it enabled me to extract real meaning and purpose in my life, and also produced significant improvements. I helped them understand, especially through my musical examples, how much they could come to enjoy that "way" of being and how they must first do it for their own satisfaction and sense of accomplishment, not for their employer. I know that you, as musicians, know just what I am talking about, and I am sure that most of you could talk in great detail about your own hard-earned skills in a way that would be meaningful and beneficial to others in non-music fields. That's a new frontier!

I explained in the transposition sections of this book that teaching our music students universal skill application to non-music fields does not require teachers to have knowledge in the other field. Similarly, we don't need to be experts in non-music fields when teaching non-musicians in their disciplines. I make the connections between my field and theirs by identifying some of the various concerns we share (like dealing with focus and patience). The non-musicians in my audiences make the applications to their specific field (transference) after being shown how shared skills and concepts transfer across boundaries. When my audiences gain the new insights these shared connections can generate for applications to their fields, they are often very surprised and pleased. Music performance is the alchemy that enables the audience to envision the new application. It demonstrates "process" indelibly. (Some testimonials can be seen at www.whatsmusicgottodowithit.com.)

I have given these presentations and workshops because I have always been fascinated by "treading around" in the intersections between disciplines; I find commonly shared concepts and ideas and then search for ways to illustrate how one discipline can inform the other. And yes, I also use it as a way to generate extra income.

Other examples of different uses for music performance in non-music fields include these: I used my knowledge of efficient movement and physiology at the piano to help factories cut down on repetitive injury claims and increase efficiency, and I used drumming circles to help executives learn more deeply about listening and collaboration. Musicians inherently already have the knowledge necessary to talk about listening well, collaboration, efficient movement, etc. and we do that all day long in lessons with our music students. So why not consider offering your hard-earned and extremely beneficial knowledge to others outside the field of music?

To conclude: We are not schooled to understand how our considerable skill sets and performing abilities can be leveraged into totally new applications and directions. But they can! I have already demonstrated it through my workshops and lecture-demonstrations.

I am convinced that my early steps along this path can lead to a whole new topic of relevance in the field of music. I call it "music transference"! There will be people who will take this idea to whole new levels and do it far better than I would be able. We can show the world that music has a wider purpose that many people never imagined. By doing so, we will expand music into a realm of usage that it has never had before. This new purpose can create sustainability and promote growth for our essential field of music. Now we have new horizons to conquer!

D. S.

May, 2020

ABOUT THE AUTHOR

DYLAN SAVAGE is a Bösendorfer Concert Artist, a first place winner of the Rome Festival Orchestra Competition, and has recorded on Capstone Records. He is a coauthor of *A Symposium for Pianists and Teachers: Strategies to Develop the Mind and Body for Optimal Performance*. He is an Associate Professor of Piano at the University of North Carolina at Charlotte and holds a BM from Oberlin and MM and DM degrees from Indiana University Jacobs School of Music.